Apologise... Hell, No!

The Power of an Apology in an Entitled World

By SJ Sherwood

Published by Blue Ned Ltd.
27 Mortimer Street, London, W1T 3BL

First published in the United Kingdom in 2024.

Copyright © SJ Sherwood, 2024.
SJ Sherwood has asserted his right under the Copyright, Designs and Patents Act 1988 to be identified as the author of this work.

A CIP catalogue record for this book is available from the British Library.

ISBN 978-1-7384744-1-7

All rights reserved. This book or any portion thereof may not be reproduced or used in any manner whatsoever without the express written permission of the publisher except for the use of brief quotations.

May I only have to apologise to my children in the most exceptional circumstances. And if those circumstances arise, may I have the good grace to know what to do and follow it through to the end.

To Caesar and Laelia.

Contents

Legs eleven 7

Part I 15
What Lurks Below. 15
A race to the bottom 16
That DNA thingamajig...25
Me, Myself, and I 34
Tailwind 46
Give me the pills 53
Stand up 62
Stick Man 69

Part II 79
Those Who Should, Those Who Could, and Those Who Won't. 79
Mirror, mirror on the wall…....................................80
Excuse me, I was first! 92
Dude, it's you! 102
Election Day 112
Gone forever 126
Denied any wrongdoing 137
Weaponised..148

Part III	155
The Givers and the Takers	155
Thank you for waiting	156
Butt-fuck nowhere!	164
Compliments of the House	172
Doors	182
Walk the walk	194
Vintage	202
Inside me	213
Part IV	227
Stick your feet up…	227
Sticky-tape and plasters	228
The last mile	237
A final note	247
About the Author	248

Blank Page

Legs eleven

It was a sunny, warm day when the cycle of life hit me like a thunderbolt from the Gods. As if to frame the occasion, it happened on the eleventh of the eleventh, at eleven am. My girlfriend had confirmed she was pregnant as my phone started to ring. I glanced at the number to see that it was my aunt.

    She never calls.

    Ever.

    She has sent me cards on my birthday and Christmas since the day I was born. I see her mostly at family events and the conversation easily picks up from where we left it last. We have that one big story that gets rolled out each year. It goes something like when I was a kid, she took me to visit a local lighthouse and told me to stay close. I then turned left as she went right. That misunderstanding almost left her stranded on the rocks as the tide came in. She was frantically searching and calling my name, thinking I'd been washed out to sea. It's funny now, but it wasn't as an eight-year-old in a room full of adults.

But for all the history between us, she doesn't call.

It's a generational thing.

I gulped, answering my phone.

I knew what was coming.

'Hey, what's up?'

'Hello, it's me. I'm sorry... but it's your mum... she's gone.'

I say nothing, letting the news percolate through me as I stare at my elated girlfriend, who is now taking a picture of her pregnancy test. My world wasn't exactly spinning at the news from my aunt. It was more an emotional constriction, fuelled by feeling guilty for not feeling as guilty as I thought I should about my mother's death. We had a complex relationship and hadn't spoken for over five years. I had effectively been waiting for an apology. One I believed I deserved and one that had no chance of finding me now.

Our relationship had been terminated as a Christmas visit came to an end. The day is chiselled into my memory. It was the 27th of December, to be exact, and she was driving me to the train station so I could return home. It hadn't been an argument in the true sense of the word—a heated exchange that you live to regret. We were alone in the car, and the confined space meant neither of us could escape. I made a strong yet polite request that she cease from a certain behaviour. She had got into the habit of trashing an ex-girlfriend and her family. Besides the fact that I found it offensive, most of what she said wasn't remotely close to the truth.

In reality, that conversation had been sitting below the surface for the best part of twenty-five years. I had spent a life-time avoiding certain topics. Historically, I had listened on, saying very little as she mocked the decisions and choices I made in my life. I had subconsciously known the dismal consequences of defending my position. By confronting it as I did, I had been proved right, and since that seismic shift in our relationship, I had grown comfortable and even confident in my decision to hold firm.

But the sudden news from my aunt had

me internally back-peddling.

Had waiting for my apology cost me a part of my soul that would never recover?

Not only had I lost my mother, but I had lost the opportunity to repair our relationship. I now had one of the classic regrets lodged firmly in the back of my throat, and I was terrified that it would stay there forever.

If our time is a series of small journeys that accumulate into our final story, then this chapter hadn't begun with that fateful day in December. It had started two years before. It was an unusually hot and dry summer in England. I was on the 149 Bus out of Liverpool Street and heading into Hackney, where I lived. A few weeks before, I had fallen out with my then girlfriend. Someone I believed would be my partner for life.

I was hurting from the break-up.

Badly.

I had been trying to make sense of my actions, especially as it had been me who had ended the relationship. There had been a series of petty arguments that had turned into escalations, which we were unable to resolve. I had become frustrated, fed-up with the pointlessness, and decided life was too short. So I left, but not before… you guessed… wanting an apology for her part in the fallout.

It hadn't come.

It wasn't coming anytime soon, and it was fast rearing its head as a pattern in my life.

If I was being honest, which I wasn't, the same scenario had lingered in previous personal and professional relationships. At best, I had a shitty attitude toward the whole idea of saying sorry; at worst, it was an ingrained negative emotional habit I was struggling to break from.

As I settled into my seat on the bus and headed home, I put on my headphones and started to listen to the Belgian psychotherapist, Esther Perel. She is a relationship expert with what I'd call a no-nonsense approach. I had stumbled upon her work via a Tim Ferris podcast and had become addicted to her series—*Where Should We Begin?* Her ability to cut through the noise and articulate the truth resonated deep within me. In her charismatic tone and forthright delivery, she casually tossed out a sentence that would change my life.

"Those who apologise first are the stronger."

Eh... what... say that again, Esther?
I hit replay.

The words pinged on the inside of my skull, closing my world even more. All I could see were the dark clouds that had been created by the episodes with my now dead mother and the ex I was longing for.

Was Esther right?

Did those who apologise first end up being the stronger?

I could certainly vouch for the opposite.

I had spent a large portion of my life demanding apologies that hadn't come and then feeling resentful for it. Was my ego so out of whack that my life was in a tail-spin all because I was waiting for an apology?

I wasn't sure, and as the following days unfolded, I couldn't shake Esther's words from my mind and decided to find out for myself. If I'd somehow derailed my life by being both a demander of the s-word and a hypocrite for not uttering it, I needed to understand why.

Was this my moment that when the pupil is ready, the teacher arrives?

I wondered what a meaningful and honest apology sounded like.

How was it constructed?

Even more, how should I receive an apology if one came my way?

I'd met and worked with people who wouldn't issue an apology in any circumstance, and frankly, they didn't give a fuck, either. On occasions, I'd stood in that same intransient spot. Deep down, I knew we were all so much more than our stubbornness and defence mechanisms, but that didn't solve two of my stabbing questions.

Why hadn't I apologised to my mother before she had died?

And why hadn't she apologised to me, knowing her last years were rolling in?

Blank Page

Part I

What Lurks Below.

"Without courage, we cannot practice any other virtue with consistency. We can't be kind, true, merciful, generous, or honest."

— Maya Angelou

A race to the bottom

My own hypocrisy over issuing the s-word had bubbled up once too often for me to ignore its consequences any longer.

I had to face an uncomfortable fact.

I was a demander and not a giver of apologies.

It had become part of my personality, and I knew it needed to change if I was to grow as an individual. I felt a touch embarrassed and even ashamed as I dwelled on previous encounters and actions. The truth tends to kick us in the core at the best of times, but I was now compelled to face it. Esther's words had opened a door that I was determined to step through or, at the very least, have a serious glimpse into to see what was on the other side.

As I began the process of deconstructing my attitude and re-framing my thoughts around how and when to make an apology, it struck me that I had no parental model. It was like a banned word in the environment I grew up in. I felt sick at the thought as I tried to recollect a time my parents had apologised to me, each other, or anyone else for that matter. I was struggling to recall one. To add to my misery, I couldn't recall the last time I had heard the s-word. Was I simply not attuned to it, or did people even care about saying sorry anymore? Had the all-important s-word become a forgotten skill, a relic slowly fossilising within us all?

Part of social evolution is that as ideas and concepts about life change, our behaviours also change. It's called 'moving with the times', and each generation doesn't want to be associated with the one before, so they develop their own rules and behaviours that set them apart. The net result of this is that behaviours or practices once considered the norm are either dropped as old-fashioned or fade away from our day-to-day repertoires.

Look at how dating has changed in the last ten years or so. We've gone from picking up the courage to walk across the proverbial room to ask for a date to being able to swipe right or left in a few seconds to choose a potential life partner.

Was the same seismic shift occurring in how people viewed and voiced the apology? Would it somehow morph into an app you could download and swipe right as a demander and left as a giver?

I had my fears.

Coupled with moving on, each generation has its own particular problems to grapple with. We've had the pandemic, a sway of sub-quality politicians, and an invasion of Ukraine and Gaza. It wasn't so long ago that Nazis, segregation, and nuclear bombs were the issues of the day.

However, one of the key differences for us compared to previous generations is our access to a computer and its ubiquitous cousin, the smartphone. These technologies have exploded relatively quickly, connecting us in a way we could never have imagined. We'll shortly be confronted with the prolific use of A.I. and it's sure to bring a host of problems with it.

In most developed countries, particularly in the West, it is almost impossible to leave your home and not see someone using a phone. They'll most likely be staring into their screen rather than making a call. For all the benefits these technologies bring, plenty of negatives ride their coattails. We're just starting to understand the impact on our brains from their constant usage and how they hijack our thinking. This gets translated into our emotions, which become thoughts, and thoughts ultimately drive our actions. Smartphones are changing how we behave, and our actions are proof of it.

In speeding up our accessibility to almost everything we consume, we've conspired to shorten our concept of time. We can now press a digital button and have that digital item delivered immediately, with any physical items delivered within 24 to 48 hours.

If it goes beyond that, we start to huff.

We've grown to expect everything in the now. Impatience has become the norm. Concentration is shaky for many, if not completely shot. Multi-tasking has become the default, which usually translates into doing one task while simultaneously scrolling through a smartphone—looking for what, exactly, if you're to really pose that question.

Likes?

The problem for our brain is that it is not wired for the onslaught of this attention-splitting that modern technology creates. Millions of years of evolution have primed us for the fight-or-flight default in order to stay alive. This digital multi-tasking world we've created is an onslaught to how we are built. Whether we like it or not, we are, first and foremost, creatures driven by our emotions. Our emotions drive most of the decisions we make, no matter how rational we convince ourselves that we are.

While many have heard of sleep apnea—a stop/ start breathing pattern that happens while you sleep and causes fatigue and anxiety, we've now introduced a variation called email apnea. If you're busy writing an email but become distracted with another task or keep stopping to check your phone, the same stop/ start disruption in your breathing occurs as it does in sleep apnea. The next time you're jumping tasks, see if you can check in with yourself. You might find that while switching between tasks, you're holding your breath at the same moment. If you are, you may be inflicting yourself to fatigue and anxiousness. Extrapolate that over the day and the week, and it's no wonder that so many turn to soft-drugs and alcohol to ease their stress.

This low-level hum of anxiety that appears to permeate today's society may not be born solely from the uncertainties of the current world state but more from our inability to concentrate on one thing for any length of time. When was the last time you did an uninterrupted task for an hour, thirty, or twenty minutes even? It is no surprise that we've seen a rise in books urging us to slow down and improve our attention and, hence, our life.

Generation Z—those born between 1995 and 2012—were the first raised on a steady drip of the internet and social media. The iGens, as they are known, were also the first generation that swapped large amounts of time with themselves and, consequently their thoughts, for time on social media. This small, but significant shift, appears to have made them suffer more mental health issues than the generations before. It will be interesting to see if the Gen Alphas—those born between 2013 to 2025—suffer the same fate.

You might be wondering what all this has to do with the s-word, and the answer is quite a lot. "I'm sorry" can take less than half a second to utter, yet the thought behind it will need many more beats. It's a thought that needs, at the very least, for us to stop multi-tasking, take a controlled breath, and then engage our thinking beyond our own self-interest and distracted minds.

On more than one occasion, I have thrown up my hands and said, "What's the point of saying sorry, anyway?"

"They probably won't accept it."

"Fuck it... they're old enough and wise enough to have known better."

"Shit happens, dude. Move on!"

I might have been right on all the above, but should that have stopped me from taking time out to consider if a potential apology should have been issued or not?

The other point I was slow to grasp about being a demander and not a giver is that it is easy.

Too easy.

"The I want camp" verses "The I take responsibility mob" are poles apart.

It takes courage to step into any battle, be it with an adversary or yourself. You need to care in a way that makes you act. And a whole bucket load of courage is required to issue the s-word, especially when we are in the wrong, which becomes its own paradox, because the more at fault you are, the harder it becomes to stand up and be counted.

If we're all too busy suffering from email apnea and demanding and walking around feeling anxious about how many 'likes' our foodie or pet post will get, how are we ever going to take the time to step back and say "I'm sorry" and mean it?

Whole-heartedly.

Humbly.

We're probably not, or not without great difficulty.

Therefore, in our increasingly busy lives, the s-word gets pushed aside and shuffled to the bottom of the pack. If we do de-prioritise it, all we've done is take a membership to the hypocrites' club because the demanders forget they have a hidden secret, too. They require and *need* an apology if hurt. These genuine apologies that come at us from time to time can be so powerful that they allow us to move on with our lives if we become emotionally stuck and hurt.

We don't want to move to a society where we can download the i-sorry app that will give us the ability to ping our response in nano-seconds. Instead, we need a moment's peace to reconnect with an inherent skill within us all. If we take that pause, then we avoid the one-way traffic and the imbalance of the demanders because once we enter that space, it's a race to the bottom, and nobody wins.

That DNA thingamajig

Our family dog is a marble-coloured Lhasa Apso. Think Shih Tzu, but slightly bigger and a bit stockier. They're originally from Tibet and were bred by the monks as alert dogs. Consequently, they have superior hearing but suspect peripheral vision, which isn't helped by the shape of their face and how their hair grows. Lhasa's don't moult. Their hair grows like ours and, if left uncut, just keeps growing.

The monks would keep them in packs, and the dogs would roam the monasteries and bark like crazy if anyone approached. A mouse, wearing Nike Air Max couldn't creep up on a Lhasa, and for a relatively small dog, they have some bark.

They're also brave, bordering on the fearless.

Grumpy, too.

Cookie is a great family pet, and he's wonderful with our children, but one morning, he bit my hand and drew blood. I think the surprise hurt more than the bite, but he's a rescue dog, and that switch lurks within him.

My wife has done an excellent job of his rehabilitation into a family pet, and she adores him. Part of that work was trying to fathom what the original issues had been. It appears that as a pup, his first home had been with an old lady. An individual in their eighties with mobility issues. A bouncy pup, prone to bark and with a tendency to only see what is directly in front of him, wasn't perhaps the best choice of pet at that stage in her life. To bypass her ageing body, it appears she used a litter stick to control him—the type with a two-digit claw at one end and a grip handle and trigger at the other.

We concluded that getting the claw part around his neck was a bit of a challenge. One that she couldn't master. However, it looked to us that she had perfected grabbing his back legs, particularly on his right side, aided no doubt by his poor peripheral vision.

The morning he bit me, he was half-sleep, and I was about to move some boxes, and he was in my way. Without thinking, I bent down to gently shoo him along, but I was on his right side.

Snap.

Ouch.

Blood.

The other thing about Lhasa's is they are as quick as a whippet.

While I was angry at being bitten and, I admit, I shouted at him, I didn't blame the dog. I knew his history and knew his trigger spot, and I should have known better. As I washed my hand, my main concern suddenly became our unborn son. Would we have to get rid of the dog, something that would break my wife's heart?

I knew that she had her concerns, too.

I finished drying my hand and started applying antiseptic spray when the dog crept over, tail down, and rubbed his head against my leg, occasionally looking up with his big brown eyes. He threw in the odd pleading whine, starting to weave between my legs in a slow figure of eight.

He was saying sorry.

And I hadn't even demanded it.

Therein was my lesson, and from a dog!

I bent down to acknowledge his apology

but decided I wanted the full remorse package.

So I touched his trigger spot.

Nothing.

He wagged his tail and gave me one of his playful barks, which usually translates into "Please take me for a walk."

He was back to the dog I knew, no longer the traumatised version who had just experienced a PTSD flashback when I touched his right side. I realised in that moment his heartfelt apology was built into his DNA, and although we're different mammals, its honesty and sincerity crossed our divide.

I was touched.

It would be hard not to be.

However, the cynic within me was tapping on my shoulder and screaming that this was nothing more than self-preservation. Within our home environment, I'm the alpha, and it's not in his interests to bite the hand that feeds and houses him. It's an obvious response on his behalf, but it didn't distract me from what I was seeing: we're all wired for social interaction. And we humans survive best within groups. Our ability to communicate and get on, to solve the problems presented to us, and to build tools to solve those problems is why we're the predominant species on the planet. Our brains have developed over millions of years from the bottom up to get us to where we are today.

Our own internal tech stack can best be seen in three overarching developmental lines. First, there's the reptilian brain, which does what it says on the tin. It keeps the lights on—breathing, sleeping, dealing with hunger, moderating our temperature, etc. Next in the stack is our limbic system. It's the bedrock of our emotional centre. Our reptilian brain and limbic system make up our emotional brain. The emotional brain's key task is to overview and help guide our overall welfare. It's there to help us stay alive.

The final part of our personal tech stack is our neo-cortex or our rational brain. All mammals have some form of a neo-cortex (which, obviously, includes my dog), but it is much more developed in humans. It's thicker, more compact, if you like. Part of this neo-cortex is our frontal lobes. These frontal lobes do the funky bits that make us human—conceptualisation, use of language, our ability to consume large amounts of data, and much, much more.

They are also the seat of empathy—our ability to feel, almost see, into another person. It's our telepathic superpower. A way to connect to others in a deep and meaningful way. Used correctly, it can give us a unique insight into another person.

The problem with the neo-cortex is it makes up only 30% of our total tech stack. Therefore, this rational part of us is easily hijacked by the reptilian and limbic system that controls our emotions. This onslaught gets heightened if we feel threatened or come under stress.

This is why, at our core, we're emotionally led creatures.

Effectively, we're top-heavy on the emotional side.

This top-heavy imbalance is both a good and bad thing. Our fight-or-flight response can save our lives, but on the opposite end, we've all said and done things in the heat of the moment that we'd rather forget.

As social creatures and mammals who possess a large neo-cortex, our ability to say sorry is a function of having the capacity to feel empathy. There are many ways to express empathy. Listening with genuine attention is one. Wanting to help someone overcome their pain is compassion. To have compassion, you need empathy. Issuing the s-word and meaning it is an expression of our ability to empathise with the distress we may have caused someone intentionally or not. We also need empathy to accept an apology, and our empathy comes preloaded within our frontal lobes.

It's part of us.

Take mental health issues, although vastly complex, they often boil down to an individual's internal impairment to interact and live successfully within a social group. It can be scary and unsettling when we encounter such people. Their unpredictability immediately puts us on edge because social interactions are core to our survival, and we immediately sense when it is off in someone else.

On the opposite side, many signals demonstrate positive mental health—hygiene, our ability to laugh at ourselves, our willingness to keep our emotions in check, and saying sorry, to name but a few. They all demonstrate to our social groups that our tech stack is functioning correctly. But in order to be rational or to show you have empathy, kindness or compassion, you need to be able to park 70% of your brain and engage those frontal lobes—the lesser 30%.

And it's not easy.

When the former British Petroleum CEO, Tony Hayward, offered his apology after the Gulf Oil Spill, perhaps he hadn't quite parked that 70% when he uttered his apology to the world press: "There's no one who wants this over more than I do, I would like my life back."

When we deny ourselves the option to apologise correctly, we are denying an inherent part of us. A part of our empathy that nature has gifted to us for our own benefit and survival.

If empathy is our telepathic superpower,

then the ability to apologise is part of that higher structure. It's a tool that allows us to reconnect when we've broken the link to our fellow humans. The more we can get on with others, the more the quality of our lives is increased. We should always be looking to leave the door open for the conversations to continue.

The humble s-word, used correctly, can save us years of missed opportunities. If we're all parking our ability to apologise because we're too busy, too distracted, too entitled, too emotional, or believe we are somehow degrading ourselves by apologising, then we all suffer.

Marcus Aurelius reminded us over two thousand years ago, "What's bad for the hive is bad for the bee."

And it's true today as it was then.

We are all better off if we can find it within us to issue the humble s-word and mean it.

So make life easier on ourselves and let it out, and in the process, we just might tap into the telepathic superpower that has been given to us all.

Me, Myself, and I

My mother had an affair with her boss at work. She was his secretary, and he was one of the directors of the company. This happened when I was around two years old. It had cliché and predictability written all over it. My mother had one doomed marriage behind her, and she must have known she was calling time on her union with my father. They had been married for about three years when she embarked upon the affair with John. When my father found out, he upped and left. I later discovered that he had one foot out of the door soon after the wedding due to their inability to resolve their differences. It is safe to say they never apologised to each other about anything. I wasn't to see my father again for another twenty years. No apology there either, but more of that later.

    I can clearly remember being introduced to John. I was running around in our lounge when my mother opened the front door, and this man walked in. I had an immediate sense of unease about the person who stood before me. Those instinctive impulses of uncertainty from a three-year-old would be proved right. I never connected with him from that moment until the day he died.

John came and went for the next four years as he and my mother continued their tempestuous relationship. It wasn't until years later that I discovered that John was married and had nine children from his first wife. Of the nine, only three made the effort with my mother and I. John was Irish Catholic and had married his childhood sweetheart from the same village. Divorce was inconceivable, but his wife couldn't take the humiliation of the affair any longer and finally found the courage to kick him out. He then promptly moved in with us, something that wouldn't have happened had his first wife continued to turn a blind eye to the situation.

By the time I was seven, three was a crowd in the house, and I got packed off to school, which turned out to be both a blessing and a source of great pain. I had been removed from the stresses of a toxic household to a structured environment, something I would later understand was a slice of luck that ultimately saved me. At the time, I didn't know any of that. I was seven and had literally been left at the school gates, not understanding until the very moment of execution that I would be a full-time boarder in the throws of an antiquated English boarding school system.

I had been abandoned, and my seven-year-old mind couldn't comprehend what was happening to me. I had woken up one day in my home and my bed, and twenty-four hours later, I was effectively living somewhere else with different guardians and different rules.

My mother had said nothing.

The school that was now my home didn't bother to explain anything, either.

As a rule, my mother's general modus operandi when it came to important decisions was to tell me after the fact, usually when I had been impacted by the event, often reminding me that I had been told. I hadn't. This pattern of information sharing or gaslighting, as it is known, would last in various degrees for the entirety of our relationship.

Another one of those informational lags

came when I was nine. I had been at boarding school for nearly two years, and the parents of boarders were only allowed to visit for thirty minutes on Sunday mornings. The Headmistress informed me one Sunday morning that my mother wasn't coming. I cried. To have to wait another week as a nine-year-old in a boarding school institution is a long time.

When the next week came, I could barely contain myself with excitement, and when my mother turned up, she came with John, something she rarely did. My heart sank. My time with her was limited enough, and I didn't want to share my precious minutes, especially as I had lost the previous week. As we all began to talk, my mother announced that she and John had married, and they had gone to Majorca on Honeymoon, which is why she had missed the previous visit.

John had now been officially parachuted into my life as my stepfather.

He was now a permanent fixture.

My heart sank even more.

My mother then asked me if I wanted to change my surname.

His surname was O'Dea.

My initials would have been SOD.

"No", I said.

That was the end of that, and they left.

Shortly after their news and in what I can only guess was the throws of their extremely short-lived happiness, they decided to buy a small fixed caravan housed on a farm in Builth Wells in the Wye Valley in the heart of Wales. It wasn't so much a holiday home but more of a cheap weekend escape, and for the first couple of years, once the winter had passed, they used it frequently. I would go outside of term times. The farm had around five fixed caravans with enough distance between them to give a sense of exclusivity.

It was also a working sheep farm with the Wye River running through the property. It ticked every box you could imagine as an idyllic Welsh rural setting.

What should have been a bunch of happy childhood memories morphed into a personal nightmare.

I grew to hate that place.

Any child who has grown up in an abusive environment soon realises that abuse doesn't come as one defined component. You tend to get it as a package deal. There's always the headline item with additional items in the cart. In my experience, it's the smaller items that create the most damage. They tend to be more pernicious, compounding the overall problem, as they creep up on you while you are unaware, piling on the misery.

Gaslighting is a prime example.

One of these cart-items within my life was my stepfather's alcoholism. The interesting part about his chronic disease is that my mother knew about his drinking problem from day one. It was a problem that would eventually kill him. Even more interesting was that she wasn't one of those characters who naively believed she could cure him and all would be well in her Disney world.

Quite the opposite, in fact.

She openly encouraged him to go knock himself out.

Whereas his ex-wife had done everything to try and curtail his habit for the sake of the family, my mother took the opposite approach. It was part of her narcissistic issues. I was to understand years later that I had become an unwitting pawn in the middle of a co-dependent partnership—an alcoholic stepfather on one side and a malignant narcissist mother on the other, with me doing my best to keep the warring factions apart, while not getting caught in the crossfire.

One of the key joys for my stepfather in going to Builth Wells, and I think the driving force behind why he bought the small plot, was the abundance of pubs and the lack of prying eyes. That meant he could drink to his own content and look to abuse me if the time suited.

One day, I had been playing alone when I saw my mother storming towards me with a thunderous look on her face. I assumed I was in trouble for some fabricated misdemeanour (a common theme) to discover we had to be somewhere *urgently*.

My mother grabbed me by the arm and marched me to the car, where we proceeded to ascend the opposite valley as high as she could drive.

She then parked our car out of sight and marched me along a path that slowly turned into a precarious single ridge the sheep had long abandoned as too dangerous to walk along. A mountain goat would've struggled.

We continued until I saw what my mother was trying to do.

Below was our caravan.

Although high up, we had a direct sight and a perfect view to watch anyone come or go into the field below. I was made to shuffle behind some ferns for further camouflage from anyone who might happen to look up. To add to the madness, it was close to 30 degrees, and my mother had failed to bring any water or food.

We each sat on separate rocks and surveyed our caravan like a SAS re-con team. I had long learned not to question my mother, so I sat there, wondering when it would all end.

I'm not sure how long we were there other than what seemed an age when my stepfather was finally dropped off by a fellow drunk. Drinking and driving was considered a game by my father. My mother both hushed me and became excited as we watched him stumble from the car toward the caravan, not before witnessing him pee against the farm gate to the interest of a hundred sheep.

My mother was elated.

"Now, he won't think I've been waiting for him to come back. He'll be wondering what I'm doing. Don't you ever tell him I was up here waiting, EVER!"

I nodded.

I knew better than to let slip our special forces mission, but her use of the "I" came at me like the baking sun. It was my first glimpse into understanding the problems of ego and what happens if you take things too personally. As we trekked back to the car, I knew I had witnessed her in a way I hadn't understood before. A new dimension had been lodged in my mind on that Welsh Mountain.

If our egos are not kept under control, we soon lose sight of the bigger picture. Everything becomes about you, and you effectively take small boys up dangerous mountains in 30-degree heat without water and do not give a second thought to the potential consequences.

"Ego" can be thought of as our conscious mind allowing us to monitor the impressions we have of ourselves. This comes with many advantages. It can help set boundaries and ensure we take care of ourselves in a myriad of positive ways—all for the greater good, hopefully. The problems begin when our ego starts running the show. History is littered with individuals who have destroyed their lives because they couldn't keep their egos in check.

My mother joined that not-so-exclusive club.

Jay-Z said, "I know who I am. I'm a very self-aware person. When you're self-aware, even when you're dealing with someone's ego, you allow their ego to live in its own space. The problem is when you engage that energy. That's when there's a problem, if you engage the[ir] ego with your ego. Then it's like, 'OK, now something has to happen.' It can keep escalating to a level that can be irreversible."

It's that escalating element that ultimately undoes us and one my parents never navigated successfully for themselves, each other, and the people they encountered.

Jay-Z is reminding us that we all have the ability to push our ego to one side. Any successful business or creative endeavour means you need to park a part of you that needs to be parked so you can connect to your authenticity and make better connections with your network and society as a whole. That's how you start the process of being successful and doing something unique.

And our s-word is no different.

As we enter our teenage years and continue to mature into adulthood, we begin to comprehend more the importance of status and power, and our egos can start to tell us that using the s-word will make us subservient. Instinctively, we know that being subservient is the antithesis of status and power. Therefore, we conclude that we are giving away something of ourselves that can never be returned or redeemed by issuing the s-word. We've somehow empowered another at our own expense by saying sorry. That we've become weak because we've uttered an apology.

Life is full of paradoxes. If we chase something too hard, it will tend to slip from our hands. The s-word comes wrapped in its own paradox, working in our favour only if we let it. If we can learn to apologise correctly, our power is greatly increased because we've parked our ego and connected with ourselves, and in doing so, we immediately connect with another. This, in turn, empowers us. If we empower ourselves, we respect ourselves, and the knock-on is that those around us will respect us, too.

That is a form of status and power.

It is, after all, what we are all seeking on some level.

Even my mother, on that day she trekked us both up a Welsh mountain in the scorching heat.

Unfortunately, she just didn't know it.

Tailwind

The relationship we have with ourselves and others determines the quality of our lives above and beyond anything else we do. Those relationships extend to inanimate items around us. Take food and alcohol. Do you have a sugar-heavy or low-carb diet? Are you a two-units-a-week person or sixty-plus? Do you own a car or not, and if so, how do you drive it? It's the same with the clothes we wear and how we wear them. Our interactions apply to everything we encounter, including ourselves, and they tell us and the world who we are at our core.

In 540 BC, the Greek Philosopher Heraclitus said, "Character is fate." It is another way to say life is relationships. Ultimately, our character determines the type of relationships we have and with whom, and those relationships will determine our fate.

My stepfather's relationship with alcohol killed him.

My mother's relationship with anger kept

people on edge and robbed her of true intimacy.

Our priorities should always be to get our relationships into a positive state as soon as possible. Then, do everything in our power to keep them there. There's no point having scorching ambition, a large bank account, and a busy life if the relationship with yourself, family, and close friends is either falling apart or non-existent. While relationships will change over time and reflect the ebb-and-flow of life, if there's a core shakiness to them across the board and they tend not to evolve beyond the superficial, then there's a good chance a review might be in order.

Easier said than done in our multi-tasking world.

My mother had her own philosophical maxim that she would pump out at every opportunity. She thought it was funny, even profound. It may not have had the eloquence and sophistication of Heraclitus, but it did have its own punch.

"I hate people. I just want to be left alone."

I don't believe this was true, but she said it enough times that it became her self-fulfilling prophecy. A mistaken misanthrope. She died with no friends of any consequence, which became painfully evident at her funeral. If you strip out the five family members, one of whom just happened to be travelling through from the USA when my mother died, there were only four other people who showed up, and they were all recent associates. Outside of the five family members, nobody had known her for more than eighteen months.

I'm not sure what depressed me the most on that day. Looking at these four people who, although they had given their time, knew so little about her, or saying my own final goodbyes.

I once braved a Sunday afternoon trying to convince her to re-think what she was saying and its impact on her life.

"But it's true", she would repeat with a smile-cum-sneer. "But it's true!"

Narcissists have little interest in their future good as they have no interest in their past behaviour. They are stuck in the present, but in a negative cycle of destruction.

Good relationships require time, and time is a key component of compounding, the eighth wonder of the world, according to Einstein. Warren Buffet can attest to that. But compounding isn't unique to the financial world. If you invest in yourself and others, it comes back to you in amazing ways, often years later. Take your kids; if you do it right, the joys keep bouncing back well into your old age.

A good relationship has its own unique tailwind, driven by the time and the emotional investments you've made. The compounding makes it easy; you're in the groove, moving forward with no resistance, but it's easy to hit a bit of turbulence every now and again. Turbulence is uncomfortable and can go on for much longer than you may like, but as any pilot or steward will tell you, it's not dangerous. And if you care about a relationship, you have to care about the past to ensure the future, and be prepared to endure a bit of turbulence every now and again.

We'll hit these bumpy patches in our lives,

and the s-word—done correctly—can keep that positive flow going or, even better, re-start it where you left off. We can also use the s-word upon ourselves. The principle is the same. You have to say it unconditionally and with no strings attached. But the key element is that you let it out. It has to become a voiced action. We can't feel it or want to do it but then keep it locked within. That's cheating. There's no point forcing it back into the depths of our guts, nailing down the lid on those desires and procrastinating that it'll get done later. We might not get that opportunity. Life is fickle, and time slips us by, particularly if we're busy being busy and task-swapping away without really thinking about what we are spending our time on and why.

Whereas generations before may have endured toxic relationships with a resigned fate, the advice now is the exact opposite. Move on as quickly as you can. If you're strong and exit that relationship, then the short-term will be painful, but as one door closes, another will magically open. We're all reminded of the lurking dangers of the emotional equivalent of throwing good money after bad within a destructive relationship.

While I know a thing or two about toxic relationships and agree that you shouldn't keep investing in a relationship that isn't working, you have to make sure it's truly toxic and unrepairable first, especially if you have some compounding underway. Some emotional immaturity or an underlying unhappiness shouldn't be confused with toxic behaviour. Most of us have the ability to move from negative positions and emotional immaturity to emotional maturity if we want to invest the time in doing so. Toxic and turbulent times within a relationship are not the same thing, although, in the heat of the moment, they might seem like they are. All that might have happened is we have entered some extended turbulence that our own behaviour could have partly caused, and the s-word will fix it just fine.

No need to shut the door.

No need to throw away years of investment in a relationship you once valued and probably still do.

Why fall out with that sibling in your

twenties and wait twenty years or more to recapture the relationship you never wanted to lose in the first place?

So many do.

History, too, is full of bitter rivals who became the best of friends. As Oscar Wilde quipped, "I choose my friends for their good looks, my acquaintances for their good characters, and my enemies for their good intellects."

Compounding isn't unique to finance and works in so many areas of our lives, including relationships. It was something my mother never understood, and she paid dearly for it. If your relationship tailwind gets interrupted and you've started to force the s-word back down your throat, then take a minute to think of the magic of Einstein's words.

The eighth wonder of the world.

And who knows what the future might bring once you do because, as any good salesperson will tell you, it's easier to close a door than to open one.

Give me the pills

Growing up, I never heard the s-word uttered in our household as either a cathartic moment or a genuine wish by my mother and stepfather to repair their faulting relationship. Their inability to apologise extended not just to me but seeped into the world beyond our home.

In retrospect, it wasn't as if the word was censored, but in the war zone that had become our home, it was like the sound of the s-word was desperately waiting for the breathing space to be discovered. They were syllables parked on the periphery of our lives, waiting to transform our environment and everyone's life within it.

Unfortunately, both my mother and my stepfather had destroyed themselves and their relationship long before allowing the magical influence of the s-word's outward radiation. What could have been a simple fix, had they bothered to pause their battles and step out of themselves, never came. It was deeply tragic, the negative compounding across their lives. They would rather walk away from any relationship than risk apologising, and I came close to suffering the same behavioural fate.

There are many reasons why we won't utter an apology. There's the immediate and sometimes deeply felt emotional struggle we have to confront when an apology is required. Those negative feelings can create an internal roller-coaster that seems to pull us down and sap our energies. It can be easier to ignore that negative vibe or turn to the nearest prop for support—food or drink, for many. There's also envy and spite, which have their own special energy. They can consume us to the point that we twist the facts and believe that the other person owes us an apology for actions we've taken. There can be the spectre of litigation that can become a reality, often consuming years of our lives, even decades, in some cases.

It doesn't help that there's no formula or algorithm to help us find the North Star of the s-word. The best we have are some accepted conventions and expected social norms, yet even these often don't help and can be ignored with an internal flick of the wrist. Life would be so much easier if we could go: the Square Root of X to power of Y = A.

> Done.
> Dusted.
> Move on.

It's so easy to do the *done, dusted,* and *moved on* bit without processing the internal emotional burden that got us to that point in the first place.

For all the power of science, it doesn't offer a panacea for social problems. There's no miracle pill for the s-word, and there probably won't be one in the foreseeable future. With the half-apology and the non-apology that have seeped into our lives, masquerading as the real thing, we could all do with a helping hand.

If we throw in our society's growing entitlement and inertia, along with our easily triggered sense of injustice, apologising is fast becoming a forgotten skill—even for those who want to use it. We also shouldn't confuse the s-word that is used as a first strike so people won't answer back as being anything close to the real thing. This imitator invades so many conversations.

"Sorry to cut you off..."

"Sorry, I'm late...."

"Sorry, I was... *fill in the blank*."

If we issue the s-word without a moment's hesitation, then there's a good chance we are the problem. Those who gush it share a bed with those who can't muster themselves to say it. Assuming we've not blanked the inner turmoil and we've stood up and faced ourselves, we're now stuck with what to do next as we blindly search for the magic pill to help us out.

To complicate the process further, an apology is a two-part action. There is first the need to vocalise it. This can be to the offended party or to ourselves—let's call this 'Action One'. Then there's the follow-up action or actions that generally need to be ongoing and sustainable to make the words we've uttered before have any truth and meaning—'Action Two.' As Shakespeare reminds us, "Be great in act, as you have been in thought."

It goes without saying that 'Action Two' is incrementally tougher than 'Action One'—note, 'Action One' is no mean feat within itself. Generally, for us to go through with our actions in any meaningful way, we often need skin in the game. The problem with having skin in the game within the apology space is that it can easily become conditional. A bit like my dog biting me. It's in his self-interest to apologise as soon as he can—in doggy terms—if he wants to keep being fed and housed. And let's be brutally cynical for a moment—from being potentially put down. Harsh but true. He has a fuck-load of motivation driving him forward.

The apex of issuing the s-word, whether being given or received, is when it beats its way from us and towards the other unconditionally.

Like unconditional love.

It's pure.

It's beautiful.

It resonates its own unsullied tune.

While there's no pill or vaccine to help us with the emotional turmoil or algorithm to latch onto for a prescriptive route, there are—dare I say—

some tricks that can help us out. The first and perhaps the most important is a mindset change. We don't need years of therapy or a month on a silent retreat to get there. A subtle shift is all that is required. A beat in time, something we can catch on a quarter breath. Instead of thinking that we're about to bleed out and die when uttering the s-word, we need to drop back and view it as something we're gaining.

A deposit in the bank.

An infusion of strength rather than a loss of status.

Once we've created this little space in our mind, the next step is to see it as a skill to use to our advantage and not a defence to hide behind. A skill we can finesse over time and even have fun with. Issuing an apology is an understated form of elegance that we can use to prove our social skills and empathy. A tool that'll be at our disposal to help us progress in this complicated world, where we've decided to swap our communities and long-term relationships for a ride on the ever-changing merry-go-round we now call a designer life.

Think of the s-word as an art form that can both sit in our back pockets and take on a life of its own. Once in motion, we can go with the flow, enjoying how it can take us to another level within our interactions. It can even become a playful manipulation thrown to everyone's benefit where we all feel received and listened to. How many marriages and long-term relationships have been saved by a simple gesture of a playful nudge and half-smile when you know you're in the wrong?

Don't think in terms of bouquets and expensive dinners. Less is definitely more. If we're expected to make a big statement around the s-word, we may have to look deeper at that relationship.

A whispered sorry and a hug can work wonders.

Try to stay clear of the electronic message sent via our smartphones, too. These sit low on the finesse scale. If we can knock out an apology in a few seconds, then at best, it's going to sound plastic and probably leave a nasty aftertaste. We have to enthuse it with energy and see it through the lens of an art form that needs to be re-learned and re-applied to our digital world.

But it all comes full circle.

We first need to park the idea that we're losing a part of ourselves in uttering the apology. The Japanese see the apology as a virtue that comes with a bow. The lower the bow, the deeper the apology. This sense of virtue is a key ingredient. Having an over-arching map of what is right or wrong is a way to decouple the emotions and limit taking it too personally. If we can put the brakes on the emotional kick-back we believe will follow, then it's all uphill and fun.

We may not be the next Picasso or the great creative at the new media house in town, but creativity lies within us all. We are selling ourselves short by ignoring this spark. If we need to utter an apology—and we will at some point—knowing that we can keep it simple and add a dash of finesse will open up more options than staying in the stubborn zone. We don't have to think in terms of 'etiquette'. We're not looking to promote a relic behaviour from the Victorian Age; rather, we have a choice to make it easier on everyone, including ourselves.

Our s-word may take 24 or 48 hours to get there, sometimes longer. But that will be better than the nano seconds required when sent from the device that has become welded to our hands. Choosing that extra beat is a win-win for everyone because we have something much better than our electronic devices.

We have our minds.

Our creativity.

And a deep and necessary desire to connect to others meaningfully, which the s-word can help us do.

The closest we have to a magic formula is our ability to take a pause.

A beat in the moment.

As Viktor Frankl so elegantly put it, "Between stimulus and response, there is a space. In that space is our power to choose our response. In our response lies our growth and our freedom."

Stand up

We can all like to believe that we're calm and rational under pressure. The truth is often different. What triggers us and how easily that thing can be ignited will come down to our personalities and the circumstances in which we find ourselves. If we care to look behind the rocks, we'll probably discover that our triggers lie in our past relationships. As the saying goes, "If it's hysterical, then it's historical."

Keeping calm and rational under pressure is a skill we have to acquire. It is earned by embracing the battlefields of life as learning grounds and looking into our pasts with clear honesty. We should embrace the challenge of staying calm as part of our life's mission. As with any skill, it requires work and practice, and even those who put in the time to gain this mastery will still have to face the initial turmoil of any triggered emotions.

Another way to look at it is that everyone gets triggered. It's what you do with it that counts.

Take Will Smith slapping Chris Rock at the

2022 Oscar Ceremonies. Smith's wife, Jada, had alopecia. It's a condition that means you lose your hair. It's not nice for anyone, but it's especially hard on women. Chris Rock made a joke at her expense in front of a worldwide audience of millions, and Will reacted. Whatever you think of Smith's actions at that moment, it was probably his emotions and not his rational mind that were driving him onto the Oscar Stage to slap Rock.

The difference between those who react and those who don't is the ability to self-soothe—at speed—in the throws of a difficult situation. The ability to access that 30% of the rational mind is the game changer. If you throw in other factors like our inclination to see things from our own perspective and our fears around loss, along with prickly emotions such as shame, guilt, and humiliation, then it becomes an acid test to see how good we really are at this rationality gig. It's tough and a lifetime challenge, but it's ultimately worth it. Putting the effort into mastering our emotions will often bring peace to our lives. It's the core of mindfulness practice. Separating that chatting monkey mind from who we really are.

Two of the hardest emotions we have to deal with are shame and guilt. Both are complex in their own right and have cross-over points, which can make them hard to decipher.

Guilt can be seen in terms of breaking our own values. If we're unkind to someone and kindness is a value high on our value list, then the chances are we are going to feel guilty. It tends to be easier to issue the s-word if we've broken one of our core values, but we still need to be careful. The apology must be for and to the other person, not a device to make us feel better. It's where our ability to empathise and not rush our s-word becomes important. That extra beat can make all the difference, even if we were unkind unintentionally.

Shame is the more destructive of the two and close to the top of our internal trigger scale. To stay calm and rational after our shame has been ignited is a super skill of the first magnitude. Shame is when we start to believe *we* are bad or rotten at our core if something goes wrong. This feeling that we are somehow bad makes it so hard to keep in check. The net result of shame is that we often begin to blame ourselves in negative and destructive ways, which makes us easily triggered. It's the proverbial vicious circle, and as Carl Jung said, "When an inner situation is not made conscious, it appears outside as fate."

That's the real problem with our pesky emotions. The more we push them away, the more they scratch their way to the surface, looking for an exit point.

My mother's particular default at dealing with her own guilt and shame was a combination of aggression and projection. Simply put, anything she didn't like became lifted and placed within someone else (usually me), dead-weighting them as her load was immediately, albeit only temporarily, lightened.

Her fate was a lifetime of dismal relationships.

My stepfather's de facto for dealing with his emotions was alcohol. Numbing himself to the point of oblivion was a common occurrence if his shame and guilt overwhelmed him. I would later understand that if he was particularly struggling and needed to prolong his numbing, he would start to mix his whiskey with milk so he could consume more without it burning through his stomach lining anymore than it already was.

His fate was a lifetime of unfulfilled ambition as alcohol destroyed one promising career opportunity after another, ultimately destroying him.

What both my mother and stepfather had in common was their inability to take responsibility for themselves. They couldn't tame their emotions and didn't even try. For them, the tail wagged the dog. Growing up, they had endured their own personal traumas, and they weren't privy to the positive mental health information so readily available today. For them, to seek help carried with it a stigmatisation that they were somehow mentally unstable.

That irony was never lost on me.

Personal responsibility directly correlates to the amount of control we can exert over our lives. If we want to be like Sisyphus and keep pushing that boulder up the hill for eternity, then take zero responsibility and don't be surprised if you find yourself permanently in a rabbit hole of shit.

Responsibility has its own calling if we're prepared to listen. The more responsibility we take, the happier and more content we'll generally be. When we're doing something, a simple check-in is to ask if this was "my" decision. If the answer is yes, then the chances are we'll be happier and more successful in whatever it is we're doing.

When emotions like guilt and shame become the dominant force, especially shame, we are apt to close down. The more we feel it's us who is to blame, the harder it is to empathise with the other person. The more you are wrapped up in your own pain, the less mental space you are going to have for someone else—and we all tend to be thinking about ourselves far too much, anyway. And if we've closed down, the s-word has literally no chance of being uttered. We've cut ourselves off at the knees, which is tragic. Because it's the utterance that can pry open enough mental space for us to step through and change our life's direction forever.

It holds that power over us if we care to

embrace it.

An empowerment that is open to us all because there are always two uses of an apology.

The one to someone else.

The one to ourselves.

Will Smith stood up twice on that night at the Oscars.

Once when his emotions probably drove him to stand up and slap Chris Rock in the face for insulting Jada.

And a second time, to issue an apology to Chris Rock, the Academy, and ultimately, his fans and everyone who had witnessed what he had done.

We can't condone the first one, but the second one is a lesson to us all.

Stick Man

My three-year-old son landed me in hot water with my wife. He did it in that charming but blunt way only three-year-olds can.

"Mummy?" he said

"Yes, darling."

"Daddy kicked the dog."

Gulp.

I force a smile.

"We don't kick dogs, do *we*, DADDY!"

Back-peddling to find my feet, it struck me that I was guilty as charged. Before the Animal Welfare Protection League knock at my door, I would like to point out that it was a friendly toe-poke. There was no yelping, tail down or scampering away in pain from our beloved dog.

Here's the version for the defence.

Cookie likes to sit on the bend in our stairs. The position places him perfectly to be able to watch both the front door and the landing which leads to our bedrooms. In general, this elevated position is his preferred spot in the house. On the day of the offence, it was 5:00 am, and my son wanted to get up.

Sleepily, I was carrying him downstairs, and the dog usually moves when he sees any of us coming. This particular morning, he was too warm and cosy and was staying put. I know myself better than to attempt to step over a dog in the middle of the stairs while carrying my child, especially as I was still sleepy with that first-morning yawn wanting to break.

Hence, the call of our dog's name was followed by my gentle toe-poke.

I didn't give the moment a second thought. Cookie joined us both downstairs, and what I had done was perfectly acceptable in my mind.

Clearly, this was not how my son had interpreted the moment.

In bed that night, thinking about what my son had said, I realised at the dinner table, I had told the story and justified my actions rather than agree with mummy that it's wrong to kick a dog. I decided I would apologise to my son in the morning and confirm his mother's statement that it is wrong to kick any animals.

The following day, my son and I sat down and had breakfast. We were watching *Stick Man*, something he loves and something I've watched thirty times or more.[1] For those who don't know the story, and this is not a spoiler, *Stick Man* (who is a stick) wakes up and decides to go for a morning run before waking his family. While out in the world, one event after the other hinders him from getting home, slowly escalating his problems with each turn of events in this odyssey-like adventure.

One of his early setbacks is when a boy and a dog want to use *Stick Man*, well, as a stick, to play throw-and-retrieve. When this little section had finished, I decided it was the perfect moment to apologise to my son. I paused the TV and told him, "It's wrong to kick animals, and Daddy was wrong to kick Cookie, and I am sorry."

That was it.

No large explanations.

---

1. A animated film based on the highly successful children's books written by Julia Donaldson and illustrated by Axel Scheffler.

No justifications.

One short sentence with the s-word placed at the end for the full impact.

He looked at me, mouth slightly frozen as his eyes chewed over my words. He smiled and then looked back at the screen for me to release the pause and for us to continue watching the adventures of *Stick Man*.

Nothing more was said.

At the risk of bringing on hubris, I wanted to high-five myself and dish out a solid ten-out-ten for my daddy skills. I could see in his eyes that it had registered. Somewhere in his developing mind, it all made sense, and he connected what he'd said to Mummy and to what Daddy had just said now. As we continued to watch the film, it dawned on me that the first five words of his life had been:

1. Mum.
2. Dad.
3. Yes.
4. No.
5. Sorry.

It constantly amazes me to witness how

willing my son is to help other children, even now as he gets older. It's as natural to him as breathing, and he's not alone with this trait in the toddler world. His nursery is a hive of empathy. There is a natural inclination from all the children to explore friendships and be in harmony with each other. When the s-word first hit his vocabulary, he would use it all the time and nearly always out of context, but you could see his underlying thinking attempting to fathom it out. He once offered me a soggy, half-chewed banana from his cereal bowl.

"Daddy's full", I smiled.

"Sorry", shot right back at me.

I changed my mind and ate his offering.

Carl Jung said, "Children are educated by what the grown-up is and not by his talk."

As a father of two, I can sometimes see my actions in my children, and it pulls me up every time, as it does my wife, especially if what is mirrored back is not what we would like or want.

John Bowlby, the English Psychiatrist and Psychoanalyst, gave the world *Attachment Theory*. He was at the forefront of child psychiatry and psychology. He built on the work of Anna Freud (Sigmund Freud's Daughter) and Melanie Klein, two powerhouses of their day regarding understanding children's minds and behaviour. They helped a whole generation move on from the idea that children should be seen and not heard.

Bowlby had been dead for over twenty years before I stumbled upon his work, but when I did, it changed my view on life. While our backgrounds couldn't be more different, and we are generations apart, we share two things that made my imaginary connection with him airtight. We were both sent away to boarding school at the tender age of seven—no seven-year-old takes that well. The second was his repeated abandonment by those who were close to him.

While *Attachment Theory* is multi-layered in how it plays out, the short version is this: a child needs to develop a relationship with at least one caregiver for social and emotional growth. Another way of viewing this is that an infant gets their confidence and understanding of the world by slowly venturing out and then returning to their primary carer when the situation gets a touch unpredictable or downright scary. It is the reaction of the primary carer and their general availability that lays the foundations of our emotional growth. Watch a young child in a playground or at soft-play. They won't venture too far on the first few visits, but their range and sense of adventure grows over time. We call it confidence, but something deeper is going on. They are growing socially and emotionally as they learn to handle the world via what they experience and what is mirrored back. The ultimate exploring is when they leave home, hopefully, full of love and confidence about the world and their future within it.

As individuals, we can either see the world as a place of hope and adventure or a dark and dangerous place. So much depends on how sensitive and responsive our prime carers were initially. To state the obvious, any ongoing abuse soon derails a child's development and can propel them into a lifetime of unhappiness and trouble.

In Bowlby's matrix, there are four attachment dynamics—Secure; Anxious-ambivalent;

Disorganised; and Avoidant. The light-bulb moment was when I realised that if I took my own attachment dynamic (anxious-ambivalent) and then took a seminal moment in my young life (being abandoned at boarding school), I could pretty much see how I'd got to where I got before deciding to change my life's course. It all made perfect sense. My need for security and a home and a family were blatantly obvious, but I was doing the opposite and fighting against what I wanted until I faced my demons.

As an aside, if you want a quick and easy assessment of someone's personality, especially if you know them, then consider their attachment style and add in a seismic event in their younger lives (a death, poverty, bullying, there's always one) and there's a good chance that this combination will have led them to where they are today.

If I play this game with Bowlby, it soon gets you to the core of the man. He was born in 1907 into an upper-middle-class family. He was the fourth of six children, and his father was a respected heart surgeon of the day. Bowlby's mother wasn't overly interested in him or her other children by all accounts, and Bowlby, like the rest of his clan, was raised by nannies. Two in his case, one he adored, the other was cold and distant. At seven, Bowlby was packed off to boarding school, a common practice for affluent English families of the day. WW1 erupted, and his father went off for active service, returning twice a year for a short time. Through this haze of repeated abandonment, coupled with a schooling system that was more concerned with producing the 'right kind of men' than focusing on a child's emotions and sensitivities, Bowlby's driving force to the career he embarked upon is easy to plot.

Bowlby was a ground-breaker, a great within his field, and one of the first to prove the impact of real-life experiences on a child's psychological development.

While you may not be a parent yet or may choose never to be, it is impossible not to cross their little paths. When we do, remember they are always watching us—parent, prime-carer, or not. They mirror what adults do. It's how they learn, and it's how they begin to understand how the world around them is working.

So, if a child does throw out the s-word at you, then accept it with the full grace it deserves. Even better, let them see you be a giver of the s-word, and not just their parents, because not only do we have nothing to lose, we will be encouraging them to see it as part of essential behaviour when interacting with others.

I have no idea why my son learnt the s-word at such an early age. I have no active recollection of teaching it to him, and my wife doesn't either, but I'm assuming we did.

Or maybe we didn't.

But it doesn't matter.

All that matters is that he can use it safely and sees others around him using it correctly, including his little sister, who likes to pull his shirt and hide his toy cars but then duly apologises.

Part II

Those Who Should, Those Who Could, and Those Who Won't.

"Hatred, which could destroy so much, never failed to destroy the man who hated, and this was an immutable law."

— James Baldwin

Mirror, mirror on the wall...

The story of Narcissus is a simple yet poignant, timeless tale of love, revenge, and death. Narcissus is a beautiful boy who comes to the attention of Echo, a nymph. She is smitten from the off and eventually declares her undying love to Narcissus, who rejects her advances. The shame and subsequent grief of his rebuff ultimately destroy her. In revenge for Narcissus' behaviour, the Gods decide that he will fall in love with the first thing he sees. With typical mythical humour and the want of the Gods on those suffering from hubris, the first thing Narcissus sees is his reflection in a pool of water. From that point on, each time he reaches out to embrace the object of his desire, it dissipates in ripples. Unable to ever connect and be reciprocated as a unique individual, he dies a lonely, loveless death, and the revenge of Echo is both honoured and complete.

The story also gave birth to the word: *Narcissist*.

Like its original mythical story, the word has taken on various meanings and a life of its own. A Google search will return numerous articles about how my boyfriend/ girlfriend/ husband/ wife/ neighbour/ boss is a narcissist. How this aforesaid individual is obsessed with themselves. It will then pinpoint how utterly self-absorbed and uncaring they are as individuals. While not wholly inaccurate, these articles tend to push a misconception about narcissists and narcissism. A narcissist may well be self-obsessed, but they don't love themselves. It's the opposite, in fact. Their inner worlds tend to be desolate landscapes. A place without light or hope. It's an utterly miserable existence for those who are afflicted, and I wouldn't wish it on anyone.

I say that with first-hand experience.

My mother was a narcissist.

Narcissism can best be viewed as a sliding scale from positive to poor to downright destructive. At the far end of the scale, you get the malignant types that push into antisocial behaviour, and from then on in, you're up to your neck in dealing with borderline, schizoid and psychopathic. Deep or malignant narcissism is far too close to the wrong end of the scale for anything good to come out of it. If you're around someone who is a malignant narcissist, then you are highly likely to get burnt at some point. And burnt badly, as a general rule. When I decided to make sense of my childhood, the hardest thing for me to accept was that my mother was a narcissist and probably a malignant one at that.

If I combined all the anecdotal stories I had, along with what I had witnessed myself, and put a tick next to the diagnostic criteria, there was only ever one result. The questions that had baffled me for years regarding her gaslighting and sadistic behaviour towards myself and everyone else suddenly made perfect sense.

One of the other great misunderstandings of narcissism is that it is a defence mechanism by the individual against their own trauma. I often wondered what had happened to my mother that had switched her from a loving toddler into a rampant narcissistic, which not only destroyed her life but deeply scorched others along the way.

I never did find out, other than I would hear the odd family story that my grandmother (someone I never met) had a renowned short fuse and often raged at my mother for no apparent reason. Maybe that was enough, and if so, it became a classic case of the sins of one generation being passed on to another.

The general difference between a narcissist and a non-narcissist is the creation of a 'false-self' in the former. This creation has one purpose only: to protect the individual from the trauma they have suffered. It's their last defensive line before imploding. Many issues accompany having a false-self, but getting an honest or straight answer from someone who has built a false-persona is nearly impossible and hence where all the troubles begin.

While people have known about narcissists for centuries, and Freud published a paper on narcissism in 1925, which effectively cemented his reputation, surprisingly little was known about the disorder until the late sixties and early seventies. Even today, malignant narcissism isn't recognised within *The ICD-10 Classification of Mental and Behavioural Disorders*, published by the World Health Organisation each year. They stick with the broader term of narcissistic personality disorder or NPD, which is an overarching category more than a specific one. Professionals will often use malignant narcissism to describe a group of destructive behaviours where narcissism is the key anchor of the group.

Our current understanding of the disorder is mostly drawn from two pioneering psychoanalysts of their day. Otto Kernberg, who is still alive and in his late nineties, and Heinz Kohut, another Austrian from Vienna. They were both steeped in the psychoanalytical wave that followed Freud.

Kohut is perhaps the more fascinating of the two professionals. His ground breaking work stems from a painful emotional place (it nearly always does). By all accounts, his mother was a narcissist. Kohut was an only child and was schooled at home with private tutors until he was seven. Said another way, he had close to zero interaction with other children and had no friends his age until then.

While Kohut married and had a child, adopting a second, he never cut the emotional umbilical cord with his possessive, narcissistic mother. She always lived close by, following him to Chicago, where he did most of his work. She died in 1972, but Kohut only published his groundbreaking work *The Analysis of the Self,* a treatise on narcissistic personality disorders and possible treatment, in 1971, when his mother had finally been committed to a nursing home with poor health. By then, she had been diagnosed with paranoid delusions.

One of the problems for the modern reader, and a huge pity in helping many understand narcissism, is that both Kohut and Kernberg's language is aimed at fellow professionals and is steeped in the classical psychoanalytic language originating from Austria in the 1890s.

Kohut also gave us the term "narcissistic rage." He explains it as such, changing his writing style toward the end of his career: "The need for revenge, for righting a wrong, for undoing a hurt by whatever means, and a deeply anchored, unrelenting compulsion in the pursuit of all these aims, which gives no rest to those who have suffered a narcissistic injury—these are features which are characteristic for the phenomenon of narcissistic rage in all its forms and which set it apart from other kinds of aggression."

Growing up in a narcissistic household, I often witnessed the pure intensity of revenge and rage, and these emotional states are the antithesis of the s-word. These continuous acts of rage and petty revenge by both my parents left zero room for any healing within their relationship.

It was all about one-up-man-ship and destruction.

Never about apologies.

Kohut and Kernberg didn't always agree on their use of language in describing the disorder, especially on the meaning of Grandiosity[2], but they were in accord on the root cause of narcissism and

---

2. Kohut and Kernberg both used the term "grandiose self". Kohut believed it was something we are all born with. In a healthy individual, this childhood grandiosity matures and becomes realistic ambitions that we are able to obtain via going into the world to achieve our dreams. Kernberg viewed it in the more traditional sense of the word in that an individual has an unhealthy view of themselves and their position in society.

when it occurs—a reaction to trauma happening somewhere between the ages of 2-5 years old.

The word "self" is an important concept—think self-worth, self-love, self-soothing, self-improvement. They can become core statements and starting points for lasting change and new chapters in our lives.

As a toddler, once we hit the two-year mark, we begin the painful process of separating from our parents and slowly realising that we are an individual who has to begin to work things out for ourselves—toddler-tantrums are there for a reason. Separating is a long and ongoing process that unfolds during our development stages and is not completed until early adulthood. When this separation process starts, especially at the onset, it's crucial that it isn't interrupted. What is meant by interruption is the onset of any dramatic or painful emotional trauma. If this 'interruption' occurs, a child can (not always, thankfully) create a false-self in order to survive.

This new false-self (note the word—self) is now their superpower, their protective mask, if you like; their response and defence to the trauma inflicted upon them. They have slung over-board their authentic, true self for this second-grade and ultimately destructive imposter. And that's when their problems really start. Narcissistic personality disorder takes root, and unless the individual is exceptionally lucky, it is going to stay with them until the day they die, as it did with my mother, the condition often growing worse as they age.

Trauma can come at us in many disguised forms. There are the obvious ones: sexual, physical, emotional, or abandonment. There's also the more subtle but equally poisonous, whereby a parent or guardian will over-smother their child, emotionally stunting their developmental journey and therefore robbing them of their authenticity. This is often called 'enmeshment' and is apparently what Kohut endured for over half his life.

The problem with the false-self is once it has been created, the narcissist's ability to self-soothe when hit with an emotional issue has been severely blunted if not completely ruined. Therefore, the only way they can manage these unhappy emotions is by constant affirmation, which translates into the controlling of others. It's this last piece of the jigsaw that dominates social media.

A narcissist effectively uses other people as a supply of emotional energy. Kohut called these people 'self-objects', which translated means people whom the narcissist views as being on this Earth for the soul existence of the welfare and happiness of the narcissist. The individual needs of these self-objects have no relevance to the narcissist. If the self-object seeks their own independence or looks to fulfil their own needs, then the narcissist is going to blow up the universe to get the individual to adhere—welcome to the raw power of *Narcissistic Rage*.

Even chaotic energy can be used to soothe the false-self and is sometimes better as it has more energy and urgency to it.

It's the purer juice.

The high-octane fuel.

Think the likes of famous people who thrive on negative news.

It's all about the amount of attention

required to soothe the false-self, which is usually a lot, and brings it to its full and tragic circle.

You can't be self-aware if you have a false-self.

The two are not compatible.

And if you're too self-absorbed and deep on the narcissistic scale, then the s-word has no seat in the house. It was jettisoned somewhere between the ages of two and five.

Narcissists will rarely admit fault, and will never say they're sorry.

I can vouch for that from my own experience growing up in a household that was dominated by a highly toxic narcissistic personality. It took me a long time to understand that as tragic as it is, a narcissist is emotionally incapable of issuing the s-word. And expecting them to is literally wasting our short lives. It's not so much they won't issue the s-word, but they can't.

It no longer exists within them.

If you're at the receiving end of a narcissist's venom, it is best to see these types in a different light. Realise there is an impairment, one that is stopping them from reconnecting and repairing broken relationships. It is also time to get real and stop seeing the world through rose-tinted glasses. We have to accept the harsh truth that these types float amongst us, and they may not be as high-profile as some presidents or pop stars, but they are still out there wreaking havoc when and where they can.

If we encounter people deep on the sliding scale, it is best to stay clear as the unhappy and the toxic have a nasty habit of taking you down with them. They can't help it, but you can. Therefore be warned, don't waste your time wanting or waiting for an apology from those who long kicked it into touch.

Excuse me, I was first!

My mother liked to shop for clothes. If it was a Saturday and I was home from school, she would take me with her. These trips were often extremely tedious, except for two highlights that made them bearable. One was being allowed to roam through the toy department on my own. The second was getting lunch, which translated, in my mind, to cake. My mother had a sweet tooth, so this part was often guaranteed, unlike the rummage in the toy department. To add to highlight #2, my mother often bought three cakes, splitting the third with me. This additional treat not only came loaded with sugar, but emotional baggage as well. Any weight gain by her would be blamed on this third slice, something she "only" did if I was out with her.

      On this particular day, we had moved to the top floor where the Café was situated, and a small queue was ahead of us. In front of my mother was a young man and his girlfriend. He was being over-attentive, which the girl was enjoying. Their playfulness slightly slowed the queue as they debated what to put on their trays. As their game and flirtations continued, I started to tense, knowing what was coming. My mother began to mutter her irritation at being made to wait.

Patience was never her strong point.

Narcissists tend to be chronically irritated, and it comes out via impatience.

When we finally got our food and sat down, my mother had agitated herself to the point of sweating. I now dreaded the rest of the day. Once her temper had frayed, it would stay that way for hours before returning to its more permanent low simmer. She stared over at the couple who were now sitting only a few tables away and declared loudly how she detested entitled people, especially entitled couples and how they should be banned at the doors.

I stared back at the couple. Thankfully, they were oblivious to my mother's maliciousness, and I was struck again with what had become a growing internal awareness of her reactions to others. Her interpretations of situations and people were often completely wrong. Her assessments were dripped in preloaded spite that had nothing to do with the situation and the person she was referring to. This man and his girlfriend weren't entitled. They were enjoying each other's company, confident within themselves and each other.

Or that's how they seemed to me.

And their confidence and contentment were miles away from the relationship I witnessed between my mother and stepfather, and their relationship with themselves. One of the upsides of being away at school was that when I came home, their dynamic together was seen through a fresh lens. What I had once viewed as normal, I was now beginning to see, was abnormal. Toxic individuals are deeply insecure about themselves, which translates into a deep mistrust of those around them and how the world works.

To add to my parent's social interaction issues, confidence intimidated them in a myriad of different ways. My mother would become indignant, and my stepfather would become mildly sycophantic. While confidence can be intimidating to some, this still shouldn't be confused with the "state" of entitlement.

A confident person—someone who is content within themselves—will nearly always use the s-word with relative ease and sincerity. An entitled person won't. The ability to issue the s-word can be used as a quick and dirty test to gauge someone's contentment level. Confidence comes from having done something enough times that you have a degree of certainty of how the outcome will materialise. In addition, because of previous efforts, you'll be comfortable with any uncertainties that may arise as you have enough prior experience to draw upon to get you through the difficult moment or moments. Truly confident individuals will understand that they have skills and strengths in one area and not in others. They'll know they know less than they think, which keeps them learning and growing. This keeps an even keel within, helping to catch and check any growing entitlement at the gate. It will also give them a baseline of what is required should they wish to learn more skills in the future.

Entitlement tends to be the opposite of all these traits.

It fills individuals with false confidence.

There is an overestimation of their skill sets. This tends to exaggerate their beliefs about how these limited or fake skills should be remunerated. In turn, this creates arrogant and unrealistic expectations. This mixture of arrogance and unrealistic expectations, combined with limited knowledge, creates all the problems. And continued, entitlement blindsides us to further information. It curbs our learning. No one is ever going to voluntarily enter therapy declaring they suffer from 'entitlement.'

Another side of entitlement that adds to the problem is that it tends to be the defence mechanism of laziness or convenience. It also sits on moving sands. What is considered entitled in one moment can be deemed perfectly acceptable in the next. Take having a smartphone. Is there a single teenager who thinks having a smartphone is entitled? Yet, go back a few years, and you'd have found a different answer to those first kids who turned up at school with a device in their hands.

It is perhaps worth remembering the etymology of the word and that it does have a positive side. *Entitle* comes from the Latin root *Titulus* meaning *Inscription or Title*. Around the fourteen century, via old French, we were given *Entituler*: *to give (a person) the right to do, or have something.*[3] That meaning stands today. If you've worked all your life and paid into a pension, then you're 'entitled' to the monthly payments when you retire. If you buy a house, then you're 'entitled' by the deeds, which you have purchased, to live in that property. It was also great for monarchs and politicians who wanted to bestow a title or position onto someone with all its associated benefits. The Earl of...

The 'ment' part of the word is often where it starts to give everyone a bit of trouble. In the English language, 'ment' is a suffix that forms a noun and goes at the end of a word. A suffix will tend to indicate, amongst other things, a state of being: *enjoyment*, *fulfilment* and our gorilla in the

---

3. Collins English Dictionary

room—*entitlement*. It's this state of 'entitlement', which is full of negative energy, that pisses us all off and destroys the s-word as fast as any politician can.

There are many definitions for being in this state, but they all take you into the same cul-de-sac: entitlement is when an individual feels they are owed something when they've not done that much to deserve it. Just because you happen to believe you're a knighted sir or a madam really doesn't count unless you've been touched on the shoulders with the sword. And you only tend to feel the cold of the King's steel if you've actively done something in the first place. That will probably mean you've exceeded the 10,000 hours of hard graft. You did the work rather than expecting someone else to do it for you. Truly ambitious individuals are always prepared to roll up their sleeves and get stuck in, time and time again.

I would like to throw into the ring my own definition of entitlement, "It is a premediated decision to refuse to apologise for an intended infringement."

We've all witnessed it on a daily basis. The

hundred-thousand-pound sports car or SUV that's parked on a double yellow or in the disabled spot because it's close to the door. The beautiful individual who doesn't feel they have to queue. The person who chips in with the 'excuse me' to the shop assistant assisting you. And on and on, the list is mounting with alarming speed. Most of us will have a vague sense when we're on the receiving end of its bile, yet are utterly blind to the same infringement when we dish it out.

If you're brave enough to tackle the entitled infringement, then no doubt you will have been met with abject failure. The reason is simple. The entitled one is already two steps ahead of you. They've long decided to break the law or the social norms, and their excuses have been well polished, loaded and ready for execution weeks before you demand they stop their entitlement at your expense.

The s-word and entitlement are completely incompatible. They simply don't gel. There's nothing that each one can hook into to get a hold of the other. The individual has deliberately shut down a part of them, even for a moment, so they can be entitled. It allows them to justify parking their SUV in a dangerous spot so they can pick up their kids from school in the pouring rain at the potentially lethal expense of yours.

"But it's raining" becomes the utterly reasonable defence. And you're the asshole for not realising it.

That's one of the many issues with entitlement is that it blocks our ability to onboard advice, or any form of positive feedback, that could help progress the situation to a better place.

How one develops a sense of humility is a tricky topic, and my full respect goes to those who confront mild episodes of entitlement in the street. I have manned up occasionally to such a challenge. However, I've also turned away, citing to myself that it's probably not worth the trouble, effectively condoning the behaviour.

Many laws and small fines aim to cut out entitlement and ensure a fair playing field for all. Laws ultimately protect the weak from the strong, or they should. Some entitlements get punished, but most don't. If we park illegally for convenience and don't get fined, then the odds are we'll continue that habit unless otherwise stopped. We also can't force humility through a fine. It has to come from within. But for those of us who work hard against our own moments of entitlement, it makes us feel the battle is worth pursuing when we see the infringement punished, even if it comes via a small parking ticket. And while that might seem petty, anything that closes the gap between entitlement and the humble s-word is a step in the right direction.

Dude, it's you!

Blame is one of the core undercurrents of a toxic household. Sprinkle it with fear, and it becomes a mechanism of control, a hard riptide to swim against. When fear and blame are blended, they keep the war-zone bubbling along, and trust disappears to the hills and stays well out of everyone's reach.

Toxic households are often spearheaded by one dominant individual who will use blame as their defence. It's this armour plating that gives them the excuse to distance themselves from the abuse they inflict by passing it onto the abused. For those on the inner-circle who could intervene and make a difference, they often turn a blind eye. This is due in part to the dominant force of the abuser but mostly driven by their own weaknesses and needs. They'll justify their position by convincing themselves it's not their place to become involved or that the situation is unfixable, so why bother? If we witness or put up with a behaviour we don't like for longer than a month, we have become a co-conspirator and collaborator in that behaviour, whether we like it or not.

Nearly all toxic behaviours come down to invading an individual's personal boundaries in one format or another. This mix of fear and blame can smash through even the toughest of thick-skinned individuals, but children or the vulnerable are easily manipulated and have no chance of defending themselves without help.

Whether at home or at work, without personal boundaries, you'll get eaten alive. You'll either be devoured slowly over time or in a wham-bam fashion that will sweep you off your feet before you know what's happened. But either fast or slow, once those personal boundaries have been pierced, we can quickly lose a sense of who we are and everything we stand for. Wars are no different. They are boundary violations by one party or several, and those bombed-out buildings you see on the news are what is happening to individuals internally.

The opposite is true for non-toxic environments, be it work or home. The key guardians ensure emotional safety and that individuals involved will take age- or seniority-appropriate responsibility. No one is passing the buck. No one is getting the blame. Everyone is taking their share of what is expected of them in a positive way. The net result of a safe environment with appropriate responsibility is that boundaries stay intact, and being at home or work is bliss.

Kids thrive.

Parents don't divorce.

People keep working for the company.

Everyone feels valued and respected, and if a mistake happens—which it will— it can be dealt with in a way that involves learning and progress.

The "fear" part is the easy bit to ignite, especially when it comes to children. Shout, threaten, emotionally bully, hit, exact a bit of revenge and the job is done, and the future groundwork is laid out. These slices of fear add up over time and sit in the room like low-hanging fruit, ready to be pulled down and used at any time by the key abuser. If you're fifty kilos heavier than the child in the room, there will only ever be one winner.

Added to that, children will look to blame themselves for adult behaviour as their small minds can't comprehend blaming their primary carer.

The glue that holds it all together is the 'blame' part, which in no time can turn into 'shame' for the recipient. If you've spent a long time being blamed for your actions, you'll often become hypersensitive to criticism. This hypersensitiveness can twist you into one of life's vicious circles. You will find taking criticism, even if constructive, difficult. Your immediate defence will be to blame back. This has an impact on your notion of responsibility. Taking responsibility means the buck stops with you, which, in turn, means you'll potentially get blamed if your responsibility-taking irks someone else. The less responsibility you take in life, the less likely you are to be fulfilled. If you're not fulfilled, it's easier to blame everyone else for the problems that you have... and on and on and on it goes.

This blame-cum-shaming recipe is mostly done via a nasty little process called projection—a weapon of mass destruction—if there ever was one.

It is a psychological process available to us all, no matter the culture or social hierarchy and it doesn't take much scratching at the surface to witness it in use. And you don't need to be three times bigger than the person you're dishing it out to to succeed.

The idea of projection has been with us for some time. "Do not taunt your neighbour with the blemish you yourself have", appears in the Babylonian Talmud.[4] But it was Freud and his daughter, Anna Freud, who helped cement the idea in our common culture. It refers to the process by which thoughts and feelings we can't accept about ourselves are unconsciously attributed to someone else. If you've ever been envious of, say, the new starter at your office, and you find yourself blaming them for not liking you, then you may well be projecting.

When a parent starts to project the side of them they can't own onto their children, it can do irreparable emotional damage. Having been a recipient of this particular creative behaviour for many years, I view it as high on the cruel spectrum,

---

4. A collection of writings from c.500 BC that became the

bordering on evil. Systematic, longer-term, and ongoing projection within a family environment, especially to a child, should be a criminal offence, but it's almost impossible to prove, and there's no direct law against it.

The one projected onto becomes the repository for all the other persons failures, self-loathing, or traits they just can't emotionally hold themselves.

My mother was a keen user of projection, not just to me but to my stepfather and, I suspect, my real father, which added to the reasons why he upped and left. It was one of the key factors why she struggled to maintain lasting friendships, as she would readily attribute what she didn't like about herself to her so-called friends without hesitation. When the so-called friends stopped calling or coming around, the projection continued. It was always 'their' fault for not calling or visiting, not that she ever called or visited them—and so her cycle continued.

You don't have to be a narcissist or

---

basis of Jewish Religious Law.

entitled to indulge in a bit of projection or be in a narcissistic relationship to be on the receiving end of someone's unwanted emotions. The perfectionist, the emotionally immature, or the downright thoughtless can all be guilty of projection, being unwilling to take responsibility for their emotions.

If you've ever had your loved one announce that they slept with your best friend while you were away for a few days, you're getting their guilt transferred to you. It might seem honest and open at the time, but it's an act of cowardice. All those soul-searching questions about how and why become questions you have to answer and resolve for yourself.

If you've been offended or hurt by someone, there's often a gap between the offence and that person issuing their s-word. While this might be hard to endure at the time, it is often the correct glide path to an honest apology and one we should embrace. We all need space and time to process our actions and emotions. But the problems arise if the s-word doesn't come. It's then we need to put on our different hat and ask why. If we're getting dumped on by an individual and the other person can't take responsibility, you're going to find out quickly that 'you' are the one who is to blame, and it's 'your fault' it happened in the first place.

When this situation occurs, it's not so much that you have to kiss the apology goodbye; it's more that it's never coming.

The other person will genuinely think it's you.

You're the one who has gone rogue.

You're the one who should be apologising.

You're the one who made the other person feel bad.

It's you... you... you.

Can't you see it?!

And the sooner that you can spot the signs of the professional projectionist, the better off you'll be. While there's no magic formula to spot these types, be wary of those who'll change the topic of debate if they don't like what they're hearing.

They'll go off-piste with remarkable speed.

I often watched as my mother and stepfather openly fought with each other, never resolving a single issue. What would start as a one-off incident would escalate and cycle through numerous previous misdemeanours within minutes of the initial spark. It would soon get to the point where they'd both be lost in a spaghetti of words and unresolved conflicts, each blaming the other, much to my mother's amusement as she watched my stepfather step onto one mine after another.

It's why you have to move fast and understand, like the entitled and the narcissists out there, that the professional projectionist doesn't want to resolve the issue. They can't. It would mean taking responsibility for those negative emotions within, and that is too much for them to handle. And if they can't take responsibility for those sticky emotions, then they'll be unable to issue the s-word, because passing the blame and issuing the s-word will never find a harmonious tune. The more likely scenario is the passing of the blame will be followed by the passing of the baton for you to utter the apology.

Acceptance is when you stop waiting for the past to be different, and if you can stop waiting for the past to be different, then you can accept in the now that the professional projectionist isn't going to change. And once you've made this mental leap, you're free to issue you're own s-word.

To yourself.

For allowing this person into your life to abuse your boundaries—probably unwittingly—but now that you know, you have the power.

The power of choice.

The power to move on.

Dude, this time, it really is you!

Election Day

My stepfather was a Dubliner who had two passions in his life. He pursued them both with an honest vigour until the day he died, and they played out in the following order of importance:

1. Drinking—he was a grand master.
2. Reading political biographies—especially those who had fallen from grace. He freely admitted (after several drinks) that he recognised the 'fallen parts' of himself within these stories. It gave him great comfort to know others had tried and failed and that he could be part of that club.

Between his two passions and my being away at school, I didn't see much of him. This suited me perfectly. Unfortunately, this all changed when I was twelve. Through a series of events, I left boarding school and returned to day school, meaning I was living back home full time. Shortly after, my stepfather lost his job and effectively didn't work again in any meaningful employment, slowly dripping into retirement and then a drink-induced death. From the moment he lost his job, his daily schedule was dominated by reading and pub opening hours. This switch in his life saw my mother even more absent from our home, but by this time, I had grown used to not seeing her.

The result of this new timetable in our family life meant that during school holidays, my stepfather and I dominated the house during the day, especially in the mornings. If I wasn't out on my bike, then I was barricaded in my room. On the rare occasions our paths crossed, he would either be drunk or recovering from a hangover. If his mood wasn't too dark, he would want to discuss politics. As a teenager with zero interest in politics, I did most of the listening. This translated into me nodding where I thought I should and waiting for that pause that would allow me to escape until I was careless enough to allow our paths to cross again.

I hated getting caught in these moments. They came across as lectures that would last for what seemed like hours. However, I did learn two things that have stuck with me ever since.

The first was that talking politics was how he held court, and I sensed a sadness within him like he'd let an ambition slip. There was an unused intelligence that had never found a home. These sessions gave me a rare insight into this secretive man. For all his faults, and there were many, he did have a flare for story telling, especially with a political slant.

The second was his story structure.

He would start with an overview of a politician's life, told as if he was standing in the trenches with them, concluding with an anecdote that foretold their downfall. He would then finish with his theory, gleamed from reading hundreds of biographies, that all those in political life would succumb to the same fate. A 'politician's dilemma' he called it. His theory went: *A politician's desire to stay in power meant they and those around them had no choice but to repeatedly lie, and it was these small lies that accumulated over time that ultimately led to their downfall.* To a degree, it was his take on

Sir Walter Scott's famous words, "Oh what a tangled web we weave, when first we practice to deceive."[5]

He would go on to insist that this pattern of behaviour was honed from the moment the politician had decided to take up a career in politics. Their longevity all came down to which lie the public couldn't stomach, or the one that broke the camel's back and finally impaled the politician upon their sword.

If someone pushed back on his theory, my stepfather would wheel out numerous examples, always able to expand in full detail, but it was *The Watergate Scandal* (Richard Nixon's downfall) that was his favourite and his ultimate argument winner.

Stick that in your pipe and smoke it!

Drinks all round, thank you!

A somewhat cynical view and probably driven by his own demons and shortcomings, but like all cynical views, it is edged with some truth. If you do perpetually lie, albeit small, unnoticeable ones, which accumulate over time, then issuing the s-word becomes nearly impossible. You start to lose

---

5. This quote is often attributed incorrectly to

your benchmark of truth, and there is no defining point from which to issue the s-word.

You are better off saying nothing.

Which is exactly what happens.

And, as any politician knows, uttering the s-word will have the same effect on their career as running naked down the street, swinging an axe, after a night on the cocaine.

It's all over.

Therefore, once you start on the lies, you might as well continue. In political terms, this has to be dressed up in palatable ways. Ways that can be fed to us, hopefully without us noticing, and it becomes the ultimate power game. Politicians, along with corporates, have a neat phrase for this behaviour. It not only justifies their ongoing soothing of the truth but negates the need to use the s-word, or even feel guilty about leaving it out.

It's called *managing expectations*.

And it's exactly what John F. Kennedy, Lyndon B. Johnson, and Richard Nixon successfully and consecutively did while reporting the Vietnam

---

Shakespeare's Hamlet.

War to their country and the world at large. Each small lie they uttered compounded the next, and for all their political and intellectual powers, they painted themselves into the proverbial corner. Each administration was dogged by a lack of forward-thinking, a deep misunderstanding of the Indonesian historical context, and a widespread fear of communism. All this conspired to first drag the US into a secret war and then an open one. It took America thirty years to extract themselves from South Indonesia, and their troops returned to a suspicious country that treated them more as criminals than heroes.

When Kennedy became president in 1961, communism and the Cold War was the theme of the day. His administration had already had to deal with the tricky issue of The Bay of Pigs[6] and the Berlin Wall's creation. When Kennedy took office, there were already 600 military Advisers in South Vietnam. As North Vietnam aligned itself with communism,

---

6. "The Bay of Pigs" was a failed invasion of Cuba in 1961 by Cuban exiles who opposed Castro's Revolution. The operation had allegedly been financed by the US Government.

Kennedy secretly expanded the military advisers to 11,000 to counter the perceived Communist threat. When Kennedy was confronted about his policies in South Vietnam and the rise in military Advisers, he publicly stated, "We have increased our assistance to the Government (meaning South Vietnam). It's logistics—we have not sent combat troops there. The training missions we have there have been instructed *if* they are fired upon, they are to fire back."

Managing Expectations.

In November 1963, John F. Kennedy was assassinated in Dallas as he travelled in a motorcade, and the problem of Vietnam was passed to Lyndon B. Johnson, the then Vice President. Johnson knew from the onset it would be a difficult, if not an impossible, war to win, but communist fever ran high, and he had his own ego to navigate. He'd become president by default—a battlefield promotion, which meant he hadn't won the election on his own merits. He would have to wait another year for the next election to prove his own standing. He won at a canter, but not before secretly increasing US military personnel and advisers to over 23,000. But he took it a step further than Kennedy by ordering secret bombings of North Vietnam.

Bombings that were executed on a daily basis.

In 1966, as US casualties mounted, Lyndon B. Johnson publicly said: "General Westmoreland's strategy is producing results. The enemy is no longer close to victory."

Managing Expectations.

Johnson stayed the term, losing his presidency to Richard Nixon in 1969.

When Nixon took office, 35,000 US soldiers had already been killed, and the secret war was now in the full public domain and under daily scrutiny. One of Nixon's core election promises had been to bring the war to an end. On national television, he told the nation that "Killing in this tragic war must stop."

Before leaving office, Johnson had ceased bombing North Vietnam in an attempt to bring the peace talks in Paris to a successful end. Those talks failed, and the war raged on. As more US soldiers continued to die in Vietnam, Nixon didn't want to retaliate openly, but he started the re-bombing of North Vietnam. Nixon feared antagonising the anti-war movement at home, which was gaining power and, more importantly, he didn't want to be seen as reneging on his election promise. However, he added his own twist and secretly ordered that B-52s start bombing North Vietnamese bases in neighbouring Cambodia. Nixon kept these covert bombings secret for months until the story broke in The New York Times. He then denied they were taking place, but he was so incensed that the story had been leaked that he ordered a wire-tap of senior news reporters in the hope to be a step ahead of the next breaking story, as well as discover who was leaking information from his administration. It was a move that propelled him into the Watergate Scandal and his ultimate downfall, and gave my stepfather his "drinks all-round" bar story.

In total, five US presidents oversaw the Vietnam War and their joint decisions and management of expectations contributed to over 58,000 US military deaths, two million Vietnamese civilians, one million Viet Cong, and 250,000 South Vietnamese Soldiers, not to mention the tens of thousands who died in the neighbouring countries from the bombings.

The s-word never once making a single appearance throughout the five terms.

If we're thinking that was another time and another place, jump forward forty-years to the United Kingdom when Boris Johnson was the prime minister of the country during the Covid pandemic. One of his primary tasks during this time was to deliver a daily speech to the nation. During these daily updates, a core message was to remind the British Public of the importance of obeying lockdown measures. It would save lives, he stressed. It could save the precious NHS, a national institution and ultimately, the efforts would protect the economy and the country.

While the country rallied and the death rate from COVID-19 crept up weekly, Boris decided to attend a summer party to socialise and generally enjoy himself. This news broke via a leaked email months after the event. The story rumbled on and dogged him like a bad smell. It would later come to light that attending parties during the lockdown was a common occurrence for the Prime Minister and the staff of Number 10.

Boris Johnson eventually issued a public apology, concluding "... I should have recognised that even if it could be said technically to fall within the guidance, there are millions and millions of people who simply would not see it that way, people who have suffered terribly, people who were forbidden from meeting loved ones at all inside or outside, and to them and to this house I offer my heartfelt apologies."

Em....

At first view, this seems an 'apology'. However, it was issued in the Houses of Parliament and not to the millions and millions of people who simply would not see it that way—a small yet important point for authenticity. Those who had suffered directly due to COVID-19 needed to hear it first hand. Johnson also sets out how he was going to manage our expectations and signals that all important political get-out-clause "Technically to fall within the guidance."

The problem for so many politicians is their apologies start from a position of being caught red-handed, clouding what they say in hypocrisy. Therefore, 'heartfelt apologies' tend not to cut it because, as listeners, whether we are paying attention or not, we tend to instinctively know two unconscious truths about the situation.

1. The politician in question has been caught with a smoking gun.
2. The issued apology has been forced upon them because they messed up the first cardinal rule of being a politician: *Thou shalt scapegoat someone junior to you.*

Political apologies often lack any real sincerity due in part because they have been scripted by a committee and churned through a legal process to ensure nothing unforeseen will come back to haunt them. This translates into vanilla statements with a jargonised tone: "Technically to fall within the guidance" is a prime example.

Most politicians have a sixth sense as to

why they shouldn't apologise and certainly have one eye, if not two, fixed on their next election, which ultimately drives their behaviour. This means they often forget a simple truth that both Plato and Confucius reminded us thousands of years ago: "The first principle of government is good example."

That's why the tribe made the leader, the "leader". They believed in them. They want them to set the tone. Set the example, which includes issuing any appropriate apologies.

The English actress, Ruthie Henshall, put it more succinctly in her interview with the Guardian Newspaper about Boris and his soirees: "That absolute clusterfuck by the government! When I heard about the drinks parties and everything going on there, I remember actually crying. Yes, I've done the timeline. While all the parties were going on, while they were snogging in corridors and raising glasses of champagne, I was stood at a window waving at my mum, observing all the fucking rules, like we all did."

When the Covid rules were finally relaxed, Henshall managed to get five more weeks with her beloved mother before she passed. Henshall says, speaking of her mother: "When I first put my arms around her, she buried her head in my chest and moaned and cried. We cannot do without human contact."

Perhaps that is why Boris went to his summer parties; he needed some human contact, too. We'll never know because he's never issued that all-important apology to the people that really count.

That heartfelt one that the nation needs to hear.

The one Ruthie Henshall needs to hear.

The one Ruthie's mother definitely needed to hear, because managing expectations doesn't technically cut it.

Gone forever

I left home at eighteen to escape the madhouse. I had moved to London and was doing my utmost to get my shit together. To be frank, I wasn't doing too well at getting my so-called shit together because even though I had left home, what I didn't understand at the time was that I had expertly packed all my emotional baggage and took it with me as I headed south.

Perhaps more miraculously, my mother and stepfather hadn't killed each other in those later years before I left, but they had parted, physically anyway. Despite living in different homes, a hundred-and-fifty miles apart, nothing much had changed in their relationship from what I could see. My stepfather continued with his daily round of drinking. My mother continued with her daily round of making enemies while indulging in her favourite past-time of thinking up revenge for the perceived slights she believed she'd endured. They continued to speak with each other at least once a week by phone and argued about nothing for most of the call. This kept them emotionally trapped and continued the negative cycle and their co-dependent relationship alive and well.

When I turned twenty-one in June of that year, I received a call from my stepfather. Seeing as he never called or remembered a birthday, I assumed it was bad news.

'Hi, what's up?'

'Your dad wants to see you.'

Pause.

As his words sunk in, I waited for the punchline. Wondering if he was more intoxicated than I thought, and I had lost my touch to spot the signs of his drinking. As an aside, I can usually spot someone with a drinking problem. I've had a lot of practice at watching the covert drinking behaviours involved.

'You mean, Michael?' I said.

'Yes, Michael wants to see you?'

Even though my real father had left when I was around three years old, his name, like two other memories of him, are indelibly etched into my brain. The first was seeing his terrified face through the passenger-side window of the car I was sitting in.

The vehicle was gently rolling down the hill, gathering speed.

I was laughing.

He wasn't.

I had been left alone in the vehicle and, in my curiosity, had managed to release the handbrake. Luckily, I hadn't locked the car doors as my dad sprinted to the rescue. Note: although it's now illegal to leave a toddler unattended in a car in the UK, it was common practice back then. Thankfully, someone had enough sense to introduce legislation.

The second is again seeing him through a sheet of glass. This one was a large pane in our front door as he and my mother screamed abuse at each other. I was crying and calling his name as he walked away. He never turned back and it was the last time I ever saw him. This moment has had a profound impact on my own concept of being a father.

After my stepfather played agent, something I never quite understood at the time, I arranged to meet Michael, aka my dad, in Torquay, where he lived. I went down on a Friday to spend the August bank holiday weekend with him. My mother had said very little about the reach-out and our pending re-introduction other than adding I had always wanted to see him.

    I travelled down feeling numb toward the forthcoming experience. I had no idea what to expect, and it was a time before mobile phones. If he wasn't at the station, I would be staying in Torquay, alone. I didn't have his address, and no return trains would get me home that day. My mother's comment about me having always wanted to meet him was true (something I had kept mostly hidden) and angered me to the point of frothing at the mouth. I believed she should have arranged such a meeting many years before this day but had always ducked the topic, projecting it back onto me.

    To confuse my trip even more, my stepfather had thrown in that Michael had only wanted to meet me after his mother had died. Apparently, my grandmother's dying request to Michael was that he should reach out and look to repair those lost years. Something he later confirmed, which did nothing for my confidence and our precarious new start. Some things are best left unsaid.

When the train finally pulled into Torquay station, I was inadvertently at the far end of the platform. It was 5:00 pm, and the platform was packed with commuters returning home and holidaymakers raring to go for the sunny bank holiday weekend by the sea. I wasn't sure what to do and was suddenly frozen with fear instead of the joyful anticipation of something I had secretly yearned for years.

I stood at the end of the platform, unsure what to do. As the platform thinned, I saw a man waiting at the opposite end, near the exit. As the crowd finally cleared, there was no doubt in my mind that he was my father. We stared at each other, taking in the moment, and I now see some of his features in my own son. It had a touch of two cowboys about to quick draw, and I can't imagine what he was thinking or what his emotions were. I was scared, bordering on terrified, and I was completely overwhelmed with what I was supposed to say. All that was pumping through my mind was that final moment when I had last seen him through the pane of glass as he walked out of my life. I wondered if he remembered that time or ever thought about it?

As we approached.

'Michael?' I said first.

'Yes, best you call me that, I think. I have another family now.'

'Sure... Ok... Glad to see you still have all your hair.'

I laughed—having hair at twenty-one is crucially important.

He didn't laugh, touching the front of his hairline where it had thinned.

'The car's in the car park. Shall we go?'

We walked out in silence and got into his car.

'Do you drink?' he finally asked.

'Not much, but yes.'

We stopped at a nearby pub that overlooked Torquay Harbour. The view was idyllic and typical of the south Devonshire coastline. He gave me the quick rundown of the intervening years since he'd left. He'd been remarried for about ten years and had a daughter and son. The son had Down's syndrome, and they were concerned about his health. My father had owned a bakery when he was married to my mother, but he had sold it to the Hovis company shortly after they'd divorced. He now made a good living dealing in cars and property and was about to engage in a housing development on some premier ground he owned overlooking the sea. He'd lived in Torquay for the last fifteen years and said he was happy.

I said very little, nodding mostly.

We were suddenly hit with a gaping pause, and he got up to get another round in.

I guess he was as nervous as me, but he came across as stiff and cold, and eye contact was challenging for him. I couldn't shake the idea that coming down was a terrible mistake and I should have left sleeping dogs lie. The truth was, I was here because of the wish of a dying woman, someone I'd never met or certainly had no recollection of. It felt like I was being repeatedly stabbed in the chest with the sharp spear of rejection. I had held this long belief that he would somehow materialise in my life, dare I say, rescue me from the throws of my poisonous home environment and that fantasy, which had helped me in my darker moments, was now completely torpedoed before my eyes.

He returned with the second round.

Eye contact slightly improved but still loose.

'I'm surprised John (my stepfather) is still around. She left me for him, you know.'

I didn't tell him they had split up, but the fact that they'd survived eighteen years before they had gone their separate ways was a miracle. John was nine years older than my father and short. He was the same height as Napoleon.[7] According to my mother, my father couldn't comprehend her leaving him for someone older and shorter.

Michael talked on.

I knew the affair had been the end of their marriage, and as the second pint kicked in, it was

---

7. Napoleon was allegedly 5'7".

enough to loosen his tongue. He unloaded all his anger at the failed marriage. He listed all of my mother's marital faults and firmly put the end of their relationship at her feet, including why he had never reached out from the day he left until now. Before I knew it, I was defending my mother over actions I had no recollection of, and it was chilling further what was already an extremely cold moment.

I don't know what I had wanted from that weekend other than to meet my real father—dad—a word I had never used, and perhaps have a fresh start. A new beginning. The last thing on my mind was to look to extract the s-word for those lost years, but his ongoing justification pushed me away and set a tone that spanned the next three days.

Looking back on that long weekend, it was his wife (and she had a remarkable resemblance to my mother) who had kept the peace and the energy going. She forced Michael to take me to see the new Bond movie at the time and a guided tour of Torquay and the surrounding area. She also prized out of me that I liked to play squash and she booked a squash court for myself and Michael to play. It turned into a highly charged game, which he won. He gloated all the way home. I have often wondered if the roles were reversed, would I have tried that hard to beat my son? Now that I'm a father, I know the answer is no. But whatever the topic of our conversation, the overriding theme was that it was all my mother's fault and that he had been correct in leaving her and abandoning the family home and, ultimately, me.

"The man who is right is a majority", said Frederick Douglas.

Douglas, who had escaped slavery and taught himself to read and write, would have seen the truth of that statement many times during his life's work as an abolitionist. Like entitlement and projection, being right on everything is the opposite side of the s-word. In economics, a theory called "loss aversion" states that individuals will work harder to avoid losing something than they will to acquire the equivalent gains. Simply put, we'd rather sweat ourselves to keep a small amount, rather than let it go, so we can earn that money back or more again.

A form of "loss aversion" takes place in relation to the apology. We will work harder at staying in our entrenched position, if we think we're right, then apply the same effort to re-evaluate and issue the s-word with all its potential benefits.

I saw my father one more time about three months later. He came to London to celebrate his wife's birthday. He asked me to join him at the Ivy with my then girlfriend. It was in a private room with the full silver service. The evening was forced, and he started to give me life advice. I said very little and, as the evening came to an end, we walked out, saying a few false pleasantries. We then stopped and looked at each other, and he shook my hand and said goodbye. We both knew that this time it was forever.

I watched him walk off, and as he turned the corner, the streetlights caught his reflection in a pane of glass from the building opposite.

Then he was gone.

As was the moment to apologise.

Forever.

Denied any wrongdoing

My mother left school when she was fourteen. If she had wanted to go on to further education, she had no choice. Her father told her she needed to find a job, and that was the end of that. Different generation. Different rules. She went into a typing pool and attended classes to learn how to become a secretary. Apart from a four-year stint as a driver in the army, a job she adored, she worked until she was sixty-five as a short-hand secretary and executive assistant. My mother rarely took holidays and often did shifts as a court stenographer during her annual allocation to top up her salary. Money that was often needed to keep our family afloat, especially after my stepfather became unemployable. Her work ethic couldn't be faulted, and I'm thankful to her for modelling some of that to me.

Her career was spent in either small firms or family-run businesses. She rarely worked anywhere for longer than two years, except in her final job. Wherever she worked, she was known for her professionalism and no-nonsense approach. Work colleagues openly called her the "pitbull", and she wore that badge with honour. She never worked in a large corporation, and I sense she knew herself well enough to see these bigger organisations as environments her "pitbull" approach would backfire.

Having experienced large corporations myself and a few smaller ones, my birds-eye view is that small companies will tend to migrate towards a pettiness which ultimately keeps them small. In contrast, larger corporations allow themselves to become battlegrounds for the ultra-ambitious, ensuring they stay competitive.

Whether you're part of one, loathe them, or aspire to run one, corporations are here to stay. Once spawned and fully grown, their main objective is to keep growing to ensure their survival. However, they are surprisingly fragile—think Enron and Kodak. Over time, they tend to get weighed down by their own bureaucratic processes and internal power games. Irrelevant of their industry, big corporations have three things in common. The first is their growth target. Despite the voodoo and secrecy surrounding it, this magical number is strangely in line with all the other corporations and is often set between 6-8%.

The second trait is the behaviour of human resources. While HR has many functions, its main task is to be the regulator and enforcer of government legislation for working practices and standards. Therefore, what happens at one corporation is ultimately replicated at another. HR also acts as a proxy-cum-modern-day union for the workers, despite being biased towards the shareholders and not the employees.

Much time, money, and effort is spent on employees understanding their responsibilities to the "corporation" and each other. Three key topics tend to drive this collective: *Diversity, Compliance, and Ethics*, all falling under the overarching *Code of Conduct*. Corporations want you to be a good corporate citizen. Should you offend someone or the corporation itself, issuing the s-word is a must. "Sorry" could easily be replaced with "survival". However, the problem with the "internal corporate apology" is that it is mostly fake and always expertly delivered by the corporate pro. It falls into the same bracket as the politician caught with their pants down and is now forced into the corner. Everyone in the corporation knows that the s-word is designed to save your job and to stop any serious internal escalation rather than solving the more complex issue of repairing relationships on a deeper level.

The third trait is the outward face of the corporation to the threat of being sued or having its name dragged through the mud. If there's even a faint sniff of an external lawyer closing in for the kill, they will either shut shop until a court of law forces them to take an action or, more likely, pay some compensation, making you sign a "no-blame" contract in the process.

Corporations also have their own "external" version of the "internal corporate s-word". This is given if there's no threat of being sued. The apology will be written by the marketing department, checked by the lawyers, or vice-versa, getting the final OK from the CEO and then issued on behalf of the corporation, usually with the tagline, "We take this incident very seriously." It should be noted that taking the incident very seriously is not the same as issuing the s-word, but the sentence is generally designed to cover both.

Escalating bad news within a corporation is like inflation on steroids and makes corporations vulnerable, because nobody in a senior position likes getting the finger pointed their way. The senior execs now have to prepare for the three-pronged fallout that is potentially coming their way—a share-price drop, the threat of being sued, followed by the inevitable individual or individuals losing their highly-paid jobs.

When these scenarios start brewing, there is only one response.

Full denial, followed by kicking the s-word deep into intergalactic space, which is exactly what Boeing did when two of their 737-Max Jet commercial planes crashed due to faulty software, killing everyone on board.

Our trust in corporations is at an all-time low. We don't trust the food or the labelling they produce. We don't trust their carbon footprint numbers or the reports published around them. We don't trust how they do their taxes. We don't trust them to tell us the truth if one of their machines malfunctions and cripples or kills someone. We don't trust them with our data. We simply don't trust them. It's a dilemma because while the trust is paper-thin, many of us work and need these companies to survive, as do the social environments in which they operate.

The film *Dark Waters* tells the story of Robert Bilott and is based on an original article *"The Lawyer Who Became DuPont's Worst Nightmare"*.[8] It's the archetypal story of the giant slain by the weaker individual. The *Dark Waters* story starts unwittingly in 1947 when 3M created a chemical called *Perfluorooctanoic Acid*, known as PFOA. Four years later, DuPont bought the rights to manufacture PFOA and began doing this work at their Parkersburg Chemical Plant in West Virginia, USA. DuPont started to refer to PFOA as C-8 due to its chemical structure. C-8 soon became a key ingredient in the manufacturing of Teflon, a Trademark product by DuPont, used in non-stick

---

8. The film was based on the 2016, New York Times

products, and one of their all time best sellers.

So far, so good.

Corporations doing what Corporations do best.

Survival and growth.

6-8%, thank you very much.

Then it turns against them, slowly at first, because problems at corporations are rarely down to one individual, making it extremely hard to spot and pinpoint the initial problem.

C-8 happened to be an "unregulated" product by the Environment Agency at the time, which, in hindsight, was a mistake. The smart folks at DuPont started to realise that C-8 was extremely toxic. It was also known as a "forever chemical". And as the words suggest, it stays in the body and the environment, never going away. The more one becomes exposed to C-8, the more it topped up inside of you.

Then things get downright corrupt.

DuPont had been carrying out tests for years on C-8 and discovered that the chemical was

---

Magazine article.

not only toxic, but it caused all sorts of nasty diseases—cancer and birth defects, topping the list.

This is the moment in a story when a whistleblower steps forward.

It didn't happen.

And depending on where you sit with the problem, whistleblowers tend to be either heroes or villains. What is often overlooked about the whistleblowers is they actively want to get the s-word voiced. They realise that they've somehow, often inadvertently, become part of something which breaks their value system. They wrestle with their emotions, rationalise their position, and come to the only viable conclusion that something has to be done. They want the wrong righted. They seek change through action and want the corporation or government to become accountable.

These are the foundations of the s-word.

In one respect, Dupont was lucky that a whistleblower didn't step forward, and perhaps a few people internally at Dupont should have taken a longer look in the mirror, but responsibility takes courage, and some people just don't have it in them.

Luckily for everyone, the brilliant Robert Bilott, a lawyer, hooked his claws into DuPont. Once he had a grip, he didn't let go and held on for over twenty years. That's tenacity. It did nearly kill him, but to his immense credit as an individual, he never gave up the fight.

As the case drew to its conclusion, Bilott still had to wait an additional seven years for the final result from an independent scientific review of C-8. The review had been funded in part by Dupont in the belief that the results would vindicate them. What Dupont hadn't anticipated was the response of the residents of Parkersburg. As they had effectively been poisoned by the leakage of toxic C-8 sludge into their water system for decades, the residents took matters into their own hands and gave an astonishing 70,000 blood samples. With such a deep and wide sample base to draw conclusions from, the results were indisputable. C-8 had caused cancers, birth defects, and deaths to the residents of Parkersburg.

When Dupont lost the first three cases, they saw the writing on the wall and settled out of court on the remaining 3,535 cases for a total of US$670.1 million, but they added the all-important corporate clause at the end.

A clause that takes us full circle in our struggle for trust.

"Denies any wrongdoing."

And, if you deny any wrongdoing, then there's really no reason to issue the s-word because why would you? And without the s-word, despite the compensation, the corporation has left a toxic taste in the mouth of everyone.

We perhaps could all sharpen our pencils when it comes to issuing the s-word, but that sharpening also extends to the corporate world, despite its complex structures and expensive lawyers working to protect the opposite. Communication is how we start our process of trust, whether we are individuals, political parties, or big businesses. What appears to have become lost within the corporate hierarchy is when they are on the brink of being sued, they will provision the funds for the pending fines, but one wonders if the reverse calculation could and should have been done. If they were to issue a genuine, meaningful apology, how much money would it save them, increasing customer trust and ultimately adding to their bottom line?

Their 6-8%.

The jury is out on whether such a spreadsheet exists in any alpha corporation, but maybe all countries should follow Canada's lead in making it illegal to sue a corporation for issuing an apology.

That's progress.

Weaponised

My mother and my stepfather were two people who liked lists. They would make them regularly and for various reasons—shopping, to-dos, personal agendas, etc. They each followed the same construction. First, they would write long-hand a random set of notes. Then, they would edit them before redoing the "final", usually in numerical order of importance, circling the top two to finalise and hone their point. I watched this process more times than I can remember, seeing many crumbled versions end up in the bin. The making of these lists was, I'm sure, some cathartic exercise, which they both enjoyed, but apart from the shopping list, I'm not sure much attention was ever paid to them once finalised.

As we continue to grapple with our multi-tasking and attention deficit lives, 'lists' appear to have made a remarkable comeback. These bite sizes of wisdom are perfect for social media. We can digest them on the go. The 5 things all billionaires do when they get up in the morning. The 8 things you have to do to attract the opposite sex. The 4 things to do to be more productive before 9 am.

We don't even have to write them down if we stumble upon a list we like. We can screenshot the post and add it to our gallery of "saved lists". While sometimes useful, these bullet points of wisdom should be used as a door to genuine enquiry rather than the finished article.

Although I take most lists with a pinch of salt, I do stumble upon ones that occasionally make me dwell on their content. I recently saw 'the things' we should never rush. The list wasn't exactly earth shattering in its content, like 'falling in love', 'making big decisions', 'not eating too fast' (I often break that one), but there was one glaring omission. And not just from the list I happened upon, but from nearly all lists flying around cyberspace.

There is never a mention of the s-word. Either as a "giver" or a "recipient". The compilers omit any reference to uttering or accepting an apology as a way to promote social harmony, career enhancement, relationship housekeeping, helping you become a billionaire, or, for that matter, eating slower. Maybe it's considered too boring or too old-fashioned and wouldn't have received as many likes. But one of the rules should have read, 'Uttering an apology'.

It's a mistake to rush our s-word, but this shouldn't be confused with not issuing one if needed. The s-word should be treated like a precious gem. Cut and polished to show its finest features, at the same time hidden from envious eyes, from those whose job it is to destroy the beauty of what we have and our willingness to share it.

The s-word's true power lies in its selective use, combined with the right intentions, backed by quantifiable actions.

All that is great, but how do we get there?

It starts with engaging our emotional intelligence. And this is the best bit, 'Emotional Intelligence' is not the exclusive use of the elite. It can be used by anyone from all walks of life.

But one of the problems with emotional intelligence is that we need all sorts of hidden skills to kick start it into action. These skills tend to sit under the umbrella of self awareness, which happens to be the most important ingredient to any growth behaviour, whether personal or professional.

On the surface it seems a strange skill to have to develop, seeing as we all live inside ourselves, but that's not how it works. We are like grand stately homes with hundreds of rooms and cubbyholes to explore. We can choose to sit our whole life in the TV room, or we can explore the other rooms and cubbyholes and see what awaits us. We might end up in the cellars and see something we don't like, but it's usually worth the exploration once we get over the shock. It's a pity, but it's surprising how many of us want to stay watching Netflix rather than go and explore.

If 'empathy' is our telepathic superpower, then we have to use it. It is our way to see into the mind of someone else. A way to connect with who that person is on a level that can build an incredible relationship and potentially achieve things we wouldn't have been able to get done otherwise. Empathy can also help you see someone's more negative traits and then help you navigate those, too. The issue here is we don't use this skill nearly enough, or at all.

If we find ourselves in a situation where we believe we need to step into the breach and issue that all-important apology, then whether we know it or not, we need to latch onto the two core skills of self awareness and empathy.

That's all wonderful.

Congrats.

Yet life isn't that simple.

What happens if, after all that, we don't want to issue the s-word? We sense that if we do, a backdraft will come our way. We can see the smirk on the other person's face. The lifting of their head, as they peer down their nose at us, making our blood boil. We know, deep inside ourselves, that if we go there, they will weaponise our apology for now and forever. We can hear them relating the story to their friends. It goes something like, "Serves them right. And you know what, I don't believe them. I don't accept their apology. I never will."

What we thought would resolve and help move both parties onto a higher plain, now becomes a battleground that drags you deeper and deeper into the mire.

I have witnessed this scenario so many times growing up, or a version of it, that I understand why some are genuinely concerned about the potential backdraft when they want to be brave and issue their s-word.

We certainly can't walk around trying to please everyone. If everyone was to like you, then you're probably doing something wrong. Having friction with others is good for us. It can keep us in check as well as alert us to dangers. With the best will in the world, we are going to offend someone at some point by the end of the week, or certainly by the end of the month and most definitely by the end of the year. Added to that tightrope, there are those out there who are hypervigilant about perceived offences and spend their days hoping someone will offend them.

If the offence is on the higher scale—an accident or even a loss of life—then there is a moral obligation to apologise. The recipient may not accept it, but there's a subtle difference between someone not emotionally ready to accept a genuine apology and someone waiting and hoping to weaponise it against you.

If we don't think the humble s-word will move us forward, then we don't have to use it. It's a choice we have and one we should exercise with due care and attention. It's a gift we have for ourselves and a gift we can choose to part onto someone else if we want.

Our agency needs to be used wisely, and as long as we're not being stubborn in order to protect our fragile ego, then it's okay to hold our apology back.

It is, after all, our polished gem, and it is sometimes best to keep our crown jewels away from prying eyes until more discerning looks can be found.

Part III

The Givers and the Takers.

"Everything you've ever wanted is on the other side of fear."

—George Adair

Thank you for waiting

It is said that the British apologise more than any other nation. How this metric is obtained and then measured seems vague at best, but if it is true, then it's certainly not broken down into what is a real apology and what isn't. And it's not the number of times we issue the s-word, but the sincerity behind the utterance and the actions that follow that count. This is true no matter the nationality or the cultural nuances involved. Like most good things, it's all about the quality and not the quantity.

We must be careful not to slip into a pacifier version of the full-watt apology. The first is nothing more than a sticker plaster over a seeping wound. The second stands you on the threshold of change and allows you to move on if you choose to do so. The problem is they can sound the same if you're not tuned in, and that's for both the giver and the receiver.

The pacifier s-word does just that. It soothes in the moment without fixing the underlying problem, often making matters worse. Those who gush it crush the life out of its importance. Each utterance is minutely damning the one before it. It not only dulls the edges for the giver, but it comes at the receiver like a wet lettuce. Damp and lifeless. Any meaning is rendered dead long before it caresses the recipient's ears, never getting close to penetrating their soul.

In the same way that our tolerance for alcohol increases the more we drink, the more we hear the pacifier's version, the more its importance dies. Over time, it turns into an irritant for both the giver and especially the receiver.

This shouldn't be confused with the quick s-word used as a non-aggressive signal telling those around you that you're not looking for trouble. It is usually uttered at speed and is a higher use of the s-word than the shadowy pacifier version. Take a Friday night and a bar full of young men and women drinking and enjoying themselves. What should be fun can easily turn into an aggressive situation if you don't observe the hidden rules. A walk to the bar to get another round or to the toilet to ease off the bladder can have you bumping and pushing past people. Dropping the s-word as you move, followed by an excuse-me, can save all sorts of trouble and open the path like the parting of the Red Sea.

We all have versions of this we play out each day as we move about society. It signals that you're being non-aggressive and allows you to set the tone for further engaged communication. We've all been on the receiving end of someone in a hurry as they barge past, huffing as if it's your fault.

The non-aggressive form fits the s-word's criteria, allowing you to be successful in society. It is short in utterance, comes from a point of authenticity, and the action that follows is in line with the tone of the utterance. Non-aggressive behaviour. We all move at a different pace in the world.

This is completely different from the Gusher. The Gusher grabs for the s-word at every opportunity, whether in speech or written communication. It's the first word out of their mouth or typed from their keyboard and sits on their breath like halitosis.

"Sorry for being late."

"Sorry for not coming back to you before now."

"Sorry, but I meant to call."

The list goes on and on and the Gusher is imaginative and inventive in using the s-word. It effectively becomes their conversation opener, signalled in the slope of their shoulders and downbeat tone, uttered before you've had time to gather your thoughts.

"Sorry to disturb you."

"Sorry, do you have a minute?"

"Sorry, but I was looking for the way out?"

In the same way you wouldn't accept an apology from someone drunk, or if you do, you know in your heart-of-hearts it means zero; the Gusher is drunk too via the saturation of their use of the word.

Gushers have another tool in their armoury when using the pacifier version, which is just as numbing to the receiver. The s-word has the same tone and construction for everyone they encounter, regardless of the circumstances. They could have robbed you, cheated on you with your best friend, or just be running five minutes late for an after-work drink, but the s-word is flat-lined like an ECG of a corpse.

The disappointing element for the receivers of this flat-lined version is that they have grown to accept it without question. We tell the Gusher that it's okay. That it doesn't matter that they're late. It doesn't matter that it took them three weeks to respond to an important email. Let's be honest; you half expected them to cheat on you anyway.

What they've really done is pacify themselves and you in the process. While the Gusher has just continued a life-long habit, leaving a tiny indelible scar within the recipient, you believe the problem has been resolved, but you'll find it lingers like the halitosis on their breath. That next email response from the gusher is… well… strangely… another three weeks late and starts the same way as all the others.

>Dear Pacified,
>Sorry for the delay in responding, but

blah, blah, blah.

    Yours sincerely,
    Gusher.

To add to the Gusher's copy-and-paste style, there's an uncomfortable truth about the relationship between Gushers and the Pacified in that they play a symbiotic dance with each other. We are co-habiting in the mutual avoidance of authenticity. While we can't fight every battle we encounter, something my mother failed miserably at, and we certainly shouldn't be looking to change anyone, there is, however, no reason not to engage your inner citadel when it comes to the Gushers of the world.

To do this, we have to engage with another powerful tool at our disposal. Like most of our free emotional tools, they need a small pause before being pulled from their hibernation and used.

This one is the "reframe".

It would be wonderful if the Gusher could get there first, but the burden is shifted towards the Pacified to hold the authentic experience in the next round of engagement. If you have waited a week for a response and believe it should have come by now, then send another email asking if the person has forgotten your initial enquiry. It doesn't have to be aggressive, and you definitely shouldn't start it with the s-word, either. You're not the Gusher here. If they're late and you arrange another meeting, it's again okay to ask them for a time that they know they can make.

As the Pacified, the Gushers we encounter are letting us know something about their personality. And like all relationships, we are limited to how many we can have, and their gushing might be the first window into something you really don't want to get into. A life of hearing sorry degrades us as much as never hearing it.

If you're a Gusher who's aware enough to have caught your own actions, then a reframe is open to you, too. Does that email really have to start with, "Sorry for the delay in responding?" If we have worked hard on a solution and it has taken three weeks to respond because of the work involved, then there is nothing to apologise for. By using the

Gusher version, we're signalling the opposite; that maybe we just forgot and have rushed it now. This time, we have given something of ourselves away. Not because we issued the s-word, but because we didn't issue an authentic version of it.

While there are some fine lines and no defined rules, the more we keep the s-word in reserve but not locked down, the better off we'll be. It's there to help us progress, get through mistakes if needed, and is part of the equipment given to us to navigate human relationships. So next time, instead of gushing and numbing yourself and the recipient in the process, try the reframe.

"Thank you for waiting. It won't happen again."

Butt-fuck nowhere!

My stepfather enjoyed telling crude jokes, usually loaded with expletives. Oddly, the more he drank, the cleaner his jokes became, something I never fully understood. His repertoire of these crude jokes wouldn't come close to standing the test of time, but one of his favourites can still be found in the urban dictionary today. Or a version of it, and it goes something like, "What the fuck do they know? They're from Butt-Fuck Nowhere."

'But' has many uses in the English Language. It can be a conjunction, a preposition, a noun, or an adverb. It's also one of those sneaky little words that tend to flop their way into our daily usage a surprising number of times if we're not being vigilant. The next conversation you have, listen out for the 'but' and you might surprise yourself how many times it gets used—but then again, you might not.

Most of us will use 'but' in its conjunction form—a word that introduces a clause—the additional bit of information which sits at the end of a sentence. This 'additional' information often contrasts with what has already been said or stated. And it's this contrasted section that is often the most interesting part of the whole sentence, getting the majority of the focus.

Take: *He's generous and extremely good-looking, but did you know he earns all his money from smuggling cocaine?*

It is safe to say that the 'smuggling cocaine' part of this sentence is going to get more of the interest and potential gossip than his good looks and generosity.

Unfortunately for us, 'but' has an uncanny way of finding itself neatly inserted after the s-word has been issued. Once the b-bomb has been dropped into the apology, the whole experience gets shifted to a different plane. Both the giver and the receiver are temporarily and often, permanently distracted.

The giver distracts themselves from their potential forthcoming actions while they reel off more buts, draining their own energies in the process. As for the listener, they suffer a moment's amnesia and forget everything that has been said before the 'but' was issued. It becomes for both as if the apology has never happened, and each is now solely focused on everything post the 'but'.

For many, our grammar rules are rusty at best. Our brains aren't going to go… oh… yes… such-and-such has just used a conjunction while issuing the s-word, but it is going to make a different leap. It has suddenly given that additional part of the sentence its full concentration, adding a whole new meaning. That clause has been metamorphosised by the receiver as "fuck you".

"I'm sorry, but I didn't see you there."

Whether we meant it or not, we've just said: "I'm sorry I bumped into you, but, fuck you, why are you standing there in the first place?"

We didn't mean that, I hear you say!

But are we sure?

Why not: "I'm sorry I bumped into you. Are you hurt?"

While the f-u version of the 'but' is the default of the narcissists, the entitled and the poorly schooled politicians, they are by no means the only ones guilty of its usage. It can slip in subconsciously to help us manage those emotionally trying moments. "I'm sorry I had an affair, but I was depressed and lonely." While the depressed and lonely may be true, the 'but' has destroyed the truth of that clause in a split second.

In our minds, the 'but' and its best friend 'however' become a way for the giver to justify what they've done, and the more we justify, the more we destroy what we had set out to do in the first place. That's assuming we were genuinely sorry and wanted to right the wrong we had created.

If we are truly sorry and have allowed 'but' to unintentionally slip into our redeeming moment, then each iteration moves our apology further and further away from our intended end-position. We had undermined our own efforts with this dropped-in conjunction.

But, I didn't mean it, we say. But it doesn't matter, because whoever we are and wherever you're from, the 'but' undermines us all—giver or receiver.

A but, is a but, is a but.

The other problem with 'but' is that it sits on our shoulders, waiting to play its crude little joke. It wants to trip us up if we're not paying attention. It's such an easy word to use that is tempting us at every moment to insert itself into our approach. Once we do, it laughs at us as we continue to use it, digging us deeper and deeper into the hole we're trying to dig ourselves out of. It's no different from stretching for that dropped item from under our bed. The more we attempt to finger it closer, the more it moves out of our reach.

The b-bomb has another advantage over us that we are usually unaware of. The longer we talk, the more likely we are to shoot ourselves in the foot by using it. Each second of a genuinely issued s-word is poised for disaster if you continue for too long. The founding father of Stoicism, Zeno, had some solid advice in this department over two thousand years ago when he said: "Better to trip with the feet than with the tongue."

Good advice for any conversation we are about to embark upon.

Often, if we feel the need to talk is when we should usually shut shop.

But it's easier said than done.

One of the biggest podcasts around is hosted by Joe Rogan. His forthright approach has had him issue a number of apologies throughout his podcasting career. It happened again in January 2022 when senior members of the scientific community accused him of promoting misinformation about COVID-19. In response, Joe Rogan posted his apology via a video on his Instagram account. It was filmed while he was holding his phone and gives a warm, intimate feel. There's no sense of a scripted statement from lawyers or a PR department.

The apology is also nine minutes and forty-three seconds long. While there is nothing wrong with the long-form approach and, if you feel this is right for you, then great. However, the longer you go on, the more likely it is you will accidentally drop in that pesky conjunction, something Joe did around two minutes in, adding another five before he finally finished.

For those of us who are looking to nail the humble s-word, we need to be mindful that we don't accidentally sabotage ourselves with the *buts*, *howevers* and *becauses*. As once they are out, they tend to multiply. If we can avoid these potholes, then our s-word will resonate in a deeper way, connecting us on a different plane.

Will Smith also chose Instagram to make his apology after slapping Chris Rock at the Oscars. He allowed one 'but' to gently air itself, coming before the main body of the apology and in doing so, skilfully avoided the f-u version that accidently trips so many of us up.

Will Smith's official apology:

Violence in all of its forms is poisonous and destructive. My behaviour at last night's Academy Awards was unacceptable and inexcusable. Jokes at my expense are a part of the job, but a joke about Jada's medical condition was too much for me to bear, and I reacted emotionally. I would like to publicly apologise to you, Chris. I was out of line, and I was wrong. I am embarrassed and my actions were not indicative of the man I want to be. There is no place for violence in a world of love and kindness. I would also like to apologise to the Academy, the producers of the show, all the attendees and everyone watching around the world. I would like to apologise to the Williams Family and my King Richard Family. I deeply regret that my behaviour has stained what has been an otherwise gorgeous journey for all of us. I am a work in progress. Sincerely, Will.

A 10 out of 10.[9]

---

9. Alopecia Areata is an autoimmune-disease where a person's immune system attacks their body, in this case, the hair follicles. For some, their hair will grow back, but not for everyone. It is deeply distressing, particularly for women, who may have a larger part of their sexual identity attached to their hair than men. Bald men can often be seen as attractive, the late Sean Connery, for one.

Compliments of the House

My mother was haunted by demons that she never tamed or ever came close to understanding. This was, in the main, due to her crippling narcissistic condition, coupled with the belief that how you came into this world was fixed and immutable. This fixed idea that an individual couldn't change was a dominant mindset for her generation, and the output for my mother was a volatile combination of aggression and emotional unpredictability that she readily accepted as the norm. Thankfully, in today's society, most of us know this isn't true. Our brains are elastic, and how we react and respond can become rewired if we choose to work at it. We can quite literally fire up new circuits within our brains that, if used enough, become part of who we are.

A large part of her unpredictability was the ease at which she would take offence. An innocuous comment from a work colleague or neighbour could have her raging for days. My mother liked to hold a grudge. She could recall with great clarity insults that had happened twenty years before. "Walking on eggshells" was a reality within our home, and even to this day, I have a deep sense of that phrase's meaning. In true narcissistic fashion, she would do her best to conceal her chronic temper from the outside world. It would be masked behind a public persona of gratitude. This fake identity could easily be cracked open if anyone scratched at its surface. And some did. But in general, she was an angel in the street and a sadist in the house. For those who have had to deal with a narcissist within their family, they will understand that pattern of behaviour all too well.

    As a boy coming into my teenage years, dining out with my mother and stepfather became something I dreaded. What should have been another opportunity to connect as a family unit would turn into the opposite. Their fallout would start as they began to get ready. It would simmer in the car and slowly escalate throughout the journey, boiling nicely as we entered the restaurant. Throughout these trips, I would remain the anonymous figure forced to tag along and witness yet another episode in their ongoing personal vendettas against each other.

On the odd occasion the journey to the restaurant was uneventful, there were still too many variables that could go wrong once we had arrived: the reserved table would be too close to the main door, the food too cold or too hot, the waiting staff too rude or too rushed, the lights too bright or the music too loud. There was always something.

I would later realise that restaurants had a strange effect on my parents. It was a subconscious game they both enjoyed and played amongst themselves. The tensions that started in the house were the leakages of their emotions about the forthcoming event. For my stepfather, it was the official pass to drink himself into a stupor. Something that my mother hated, was embarrassed by, yet secretly encouraged. For my mother, she could indulge in her favourite sponge-and-cream heavy desserts. She nearly always ordered two and would rush to eat her mains to get to her desired prize. It was a habit that my stepfather would use to moan at the additional cost when the bill came, yet it gave him the golden ammunition he needed to pick on her fluctuating weight.

Endless.

During these 'dining hells', my mother would often find a fake reason to demand an apology from the establishment in question. If we were moved tables and she wasn't apologised to for the infringement in play, then the gesture to move didn't count. After witnessing this circus act for years, I started to see the subtext in her demands. She wasn't interested one iota in receiving the s-word from anyone within the service industry (or anyone for that matter). Its healing effects were lost on her, as she had never issued an apology in her life, therefore, there was little value in receiving one from someone else. What would she do with it, anyway? It would mean that she would need to process complex emotions and their meaning, and then consider another human being and their point of view. These were skills she didn't possess or was even interested in acquiring.

Her ruse amounted to a side hustle, which she deemed lucrative. Her demand for the s-word for anything related to the service industry was highly manipulative on her part and had one reason only.

It was an understated demand for compensation.

And it needed to be subtle because, for most, including my mother, there's an uneasy fit between the s-word and a meaningful action that follows, or the s-word that is aimed at being topped up with compensation.

Hang on... I hear you shout.

Compensation for a wrong is an action.

Well... technically, yes, but it should be viewed as the 'secondary action' and not the 'primary'.

Context becomes the key. If we were to lose a leg through neglect by an individual or workplace incident, then the s-word is a must to allow us to come to terms with the emotional stress and life-changing event that has happened. The compensation is the secondary action. It is to assist us and ease the challenges ahead for the life-changing injury we've suffered. The sequence of events becomes crucial. The right order is needed for us to ensure closure and move on with our lives. If we suffer a life-changing event through no fault of our own and only receive the compensation and not the apology, it will eat away at us despite the million or so in the bank.

To state the obvious, any life-changing injury is not on the same spectrum as having our restaurant table double-booked, our anniversary bombed by a careless error, or the waiter spilling red wine on our clothes. But if we're not careful, we can view these incidents as if they are. The problem we encounter is really with our egos that have become bruised. At that moment, the free bottle of wine becomes as important as the large payout with the zeros and the commas. The food that arrives cold feels like we've lost our leg.

If our s-word requirement becomes a secret cry for a free lunch, then be warned. There's nothing free in life and the next time we find ourselves angling for that freebie for a mistake by the service industry, check in again with yourself. Are you secretly conflating the s-word and the all-important proceeding action, focused only on the 'secondary action'? The compensation part, when what we should be doing is keeping three distinct silos.

>Apology.

>Action.

>Compensation—not mandatory unless we've suffered a life-changing incident or specific circumstances require financial recompense.

If we've ever found ourselves tricked or conned out of something, then there's that awful moment when the truth rushes in. It comes in like a giant emotional wave, moving us from the heat of embarrassment to the harsh lessons of reality, hopefully settling on wisdom to be used in the future.

Part of that gamut of emotions is a feeling of emptiness at our own stupidity, focused on the loss of the thing we've been tricked out of, usually money. It's the same with the free lunch syndrome, which comes at the expense of the s-word and the proceeding actions. Without realising, we've demanded an apology in the form of a materialistic item, and while the restaurant manager will magically find you a table (or usually), the s-word is rushed, even made on the move through a half turn as they scurry away.

Then, as we sit at our new table, the free bottle of red or white is produced, followed by the famous words:

"Compliments of the House."

The wine is corked, and all is forgiven and forgotten.

Or is it?

Don't be surprised if a nagging feeling of discontent arises inside; our emotions unable to settle. There's a flicker of a thought in the peripheries of our mind telling us this it isn't quite resolved. While we might discuss the whole incident with our dining partner and confirm the fact they should have given the freebie, we'll notice that the problem hasn't quite gone away, at least not psychologically.

That itch hasn't been scratched.

That hole hasn't been filled.

We've mugged ourselves off without even

realising what we've done.

Hopefully, we are not going to throw an apology or the freebie back at someone to shame them, but we need to tread carefully so that we don't effectively do the equivalent to ourselves. This freebie has unintentionally morphed into a compromise. What we were looking for was the correct order of events. This hasn't happened partly because greed has appeared on the horizon, along with our inability to negotiate successfully. Most of us are poor negotiators because it's a skill we need to practice, and we confuse stubbornness or a loud voice with negotiation. Both are signalling our inability to think around and beyond the problem at hand.

Negotiating even the simple things can be difficult and compromise is overrated, especially if it is rushed into. We need to ask ourselves, do we really need that free bottle of wine over the more important s-word and actions that will—if not immediately—leave a longer-term psychological balance and recompense than any quick fix will?

If being cautious of a free lunch is good

advice, then being wary of *Compliments of the House* is another one to watch out for.

Our aim should be to leave that restaurant with our dignity and psychological well-being intact and not a free bottle of wine that maybe you didn't want in the first place.

Doors

Monsters Inc. is an animated movie by Pixar and follows Sully—a blue Yeti-type monster—who is an expert scarer. Being a "scarer" is a highly skilled and important job in Monstropolis, as monsters need to harness the screams of children for "energy". This is considered a dangerous job for Sully and the other expert scarers, as children are believed to be highly toxic and are becoming harder and harder to scare. Access from the Monster's World into the human world is done via special portals, or doors, that are inserted in the wardrobes of children's bedrooms.

> So far, so good.
>
> But not for long!
>
> One evening, Sully discovers an 'active' door has been left open at a rival's factory in Monstropolis. Sully goes to inspect the door and inadvertently lets a toddler into the factory and into Monster World.
>
> Oops.
>
> Chaos ensues—that's toddlers for you.

The inventive use of the doors, a toddler running wild in Monstropolis, and the rivalry between the two competing firms make for a wonderfully animated movie. It was a movie I had no intention of watching and saw by accident on a long-haul flight. The minute it started, I was hooked. Apart from the inventive script, I had my own secret obsession with doors, or more to the point, the entering and the exiting of them.

In the domestic war zone I had grown up in, the sound of a door opening and closing became my own portal into the moods of my parents. We effectively had two front doors. A small porch at the front with a door, followed by the main door into our home. I became an adept interpreter of the energy that followed the opening of these two doors. The combined sound was like a pre-warning followed by the main alarm. Amber to red, or amber to green. I felt like one of those Native American Indians who could taste the wind and sense what was coming—a hurricane or a summer breeze. I could literally tell by how the front doors were opened how drunk my stepfather was—two, three attempts at the key spoke volumes. How hard the door was pushed, how his foot scraped the threshold. Then, there was the speed at which my mother would enter. I could map it on a scale of 1-10, gauging her levels of anger. The sound of these doors would immediately let me know if I needed to barricade myself into my bedroom or not—something I frequently did—or if I could exit through my own bedroom door and join our disconnected family for the odd moments of peace. On more than one occasion, I had slipped out of the back door as the porch door opened, only to climb over our garage roof, come through the front door, and head up the stairs to my bedroom, effectively avoiding being caught downstairs.

As I moved into my teens, my fascination with doors expanded beyond the emotions of those comings and goings. I don't know why, but I had added a financial element to my game. Surviving on meagre pocket money, a paper round, and a Saturday job in an Indian Restaurant, I started to think of the personal cost or upside of every time I entered through a door. Was I going to spend money or get paid if I entered this place? At the time, I worked out that, on average, it cost me around £2 for every door I entered. This was an astronomical sum in relation to what I was earning, and in order to save money, I needed to be more discerning about which doors I entered or didn't.

It was a fun game at the time, which I still occasionally play. Another door I stepped through gave me one of the best returns ever, and it happened toward the end of my twenties. I entered a local café, not one of those sophisticated coffee houses of today, but more a greasy spoon full of builders and drivers. Hung on the wall in a dirty and broken fake beechwood frame was a quote.

> "Character is fate."
> —Heraclitus

I had zero idea who Heraclitus was, but the quote hit me between the eyes with the force of a thrown brick. I had always assumed 'fate' was something that just happened to you. You had no say in it. It was either good or bad. The idea that our 'character' or the things that we think, do, and say, can be changed at any time, were the determining factors in what happened to us was utterly revolutionary to me. The concept that any one of us could simply change our thoughts, which in turn could change our actions, then, in turn, change our character and ultimately our fate, struck me as the magic formula to life—something I have since proved to myself over and over again on countless occasions.

As these thoughts percolated through me, I started to think of the quote in regards to my mother and stepfather and their life choices. It was the first time their behaviours started to make sense to me. I could see the lineage of their actions. In many ways, it was also the start of my own personal growth story. I'd had a couple of false starts before that moment, but seeing this quote turned me in another direction, helping me draw a line in the sand.

What I didn't know at the time was the quote was from Ancient Greek Philosophy. The birth of Greek philosophy started in Miletus around 1000

BC, which was then part of the ancient Ionia region of Greece, now Turkey. Heraclitus was an Ionian. Ancient Greek cities were effectively city-states, ruled by themselves, and Miletus became super rich through its trading and industry mostly with the Egyptians. Once rich, and flooded with diversity, the city excelled in literature, philosophy, and art. This heady mix, supported by its wealth, helped develop two of the most famous Greek gifts to the world: science and philosophy.

Over time, Ancient Greek Philosophy developed many schools of thought: Epicureanism, Cynicism, Pythagoreans, and Stoicism. Stoic philosophy is perhaps the most famous and was founded by Zeno of Citium, which was a thriving seaport in Southern Cyprus near the beautiful town of Larnaca. In many ways, Stoicism is the last effort of the Greeks, prior to Christianity, to establish a moral ethic by which to live by.

Zeno, by all accounts, was a rich merchant on his way to Athens who got caught in a storm and was shipwrecked, losing his fortune in the process. Surviving his ordeal, he arrives in Athens and sitting down at bookseller's stall, he begins to read Xenophon's *Memorabilia* and is fascinated by the character of Socrates. He asks where he can find such a man and, as luck would have it, Crates, a Cynic philosopher, passes by. The Bookseller told Zeno to follow that man, and his questions would be answered. The world is thankful that he did, and after studying under Crates for many years, he set up his own school, discussing informally his philosophic ideas as he walked along the covered colonnades of the Stoa Poikile, or The Painted Porch, and Stoicism was born.

The far-reaching ethics of stoicism is almost impossible to quantify, but it drove its way into Rome, creating a lasting legacy with the men it touched. Marcus Aurelius, Cato, and Seneca are some of its most famous recipients, and Seneca is perhaps the more complex of the three. Born into the upper classes, he was schooled in the disciplines expected of him, and one of those included Greek Philosophy. A life amongst the elite in politics and law was a given.

The period he is perhaps most famous for

didn't start until his mid-fifties and began when he was brought back from exile to school the then twelve-year old Nero. Seneca's remit was straightforward enough. He was to be to Nero what Aristotle was to Alexander the Great. He was to turn the young man into a great Roman Emperor and leader of men.

      Over the next fifteen years, Seneca would witness Nero descend into a paranoid madness, sexual perversity, bloated from indulgences, a man more concerned with his singing and dancing than becoming a great emperor. During Seneca's watch, Nero killed five members of his family, including his mother and his first wife. As his personal tutor, Seneca was said to be able to moderate some of Nero's more murderous traits, but it also meant that he had either willingly, or not, colluded with the regime and enriched himself in the process. Seneca became exceedingly rich, mostly through the financing scheme he set up to fund the invasion of Britannia, something he was able to do from his elevated position within the Senate and was common practise for individuals with these privileges.

It is extremely difficult to judge the behaviours of antiquity through a modern lens, and Seneca lived in a world where getting sacked often meant exile or death. He may have had an impossible job, especially when considering Nero's heritage and mental instability. However, our environments greatly impact our lives, and even the great Seneca couldn't escape that fate. The fifteen years he spent in Nero's inner circle effectively killed him. And, for all his brilliance, he slowly corrupted his values, becoming one of history's most fascinating hypocrites that has let to endless speculation about the character of the man.

In Seneca's letters to his friend, Lucilius, his advice comes at you like a man apologising to himself as much as passing on his wisdom from the unique and hard-fought world of ancient Rome politics. Taken in the context of failing at his primary task of schooling Nero and corrupting himself in the process, his words take on a deeper meaning:

"Of this one thing, make sure against your

dying day—that your faults die before you do."

"It is not the man who has too little that is poor, but the one who hankers after more."

"To win true freedom, you must be a slave to philosophy."

The last one is interesting in that Seneca wasn't a philosopher in the sense of Zeno or Epictetus in that he set up his own school and dedicated his life to philosophy, but he was a man deeply schooled in its strengths and ethics, but was unable to always live up to those lofty ambitions.

At times, Seneca is like the alcoholic who, despite attending Alcoholics Anonymous and watching his personal and professional life implode, keeps reaching for that next drink.

"One more, and I'll stop," I often heard my stepfather say.

Seneca must have known early on that the signs for his success with Nero didn't bode well, yet he continued. Maybe he thought he'd win in the end, or maybe the power he'd always craved was too much to walk away from now that he'd been given that final chance at such a late stage in his life. Ultimately, he wasn't a slave enough to his own philosophy, and it cost him.

We may not have the eloquence and insight of Seneca, but we each have the gift to apologise to ourselves. We can do this at any time and there's no need to wait until the end portion of our lives. And the rules for issuing the apology stay the same whether you're issuing the s-word to someone else or to yourself. We first have to acknowledge the situation we are in may be down to our own doing and that we will have to deal with those uncomfortable emotions that arise from the realisation. Once we do, we can issue the s-word to ourselves, becoming both the "Giver" and the "Taker" in one. A unique position and one we should embrace. Then, the action is laid at our own feet to take. Stoicism at its best – it's within our control and nobody else's.

We're now at the threshold of the door we've opened. We can step through it or not. We have presented ourselves with an opportunity for personal forgiveness, a moment to be compassionate with who we are and witness that kind and honest small child within who has probably been hiding away for years.

>That's the power of the humble s-word.
>
>It stands us at the door of choice.
>
>We can step through, or not.
>
>And if we're unsure what to do next, then

some more stoic advice from the 3rd Century BC might help.

>Memento Mori.
>
>Remember you will die.

Walk the walk

The pub where my stepfather did most of his drinking was called *The Chase*. It was close to a small junction and set back from the main road. I would often walk by, either heading home or into our small town, and peer inside to see him drinking. He would do his best to hold court with one of his political tales, but as time went on, I saw him more and more alone, either standing at the bar or sitting at a small round table, staring into his drink. The slackness in his face and the distant glaze in his eyes said it all. His life was a catalogue of regrets that he would ruminate on, and his mechanism for coping was alcohol. To this day, if I walk past a pub and see an older man sitting at a table alone, staring into a drink, it overwhelms me with a sense of sadness.

Over the years, he would sometimes let slip the inner turmoil driving him out of the house and into *The Chase*. I could also see with my own eyes the demons that hung on his shoulders. The abandonment of his first wife, his childhood sweetheart, and their nine children. My mother and stepfather were better as a couple having an affair than they ever were as husband and wife. So much pain would have been averted had they kept their relationship there. His sexuality was another issue (he had latent homosexual issues and was born at a time when it was still a crime to be sexually orientated in that way). The death of his two brothers. The poor relationship with four of his children, who refused to see him. His ability to destroy one good job after another trailed him his whole life. Added into the mix was his religion. He was Irish Catholic and suffered all the guilty feelings that his religious upbringing had dumped upon him, dropping him into periods of penance.

For him, penance was his unvoiced apology and coincided with him taking a sabbatical from the drink. While we can choose to do penance voluntarily, it can be ordered upon us. Many religions include penance as a way to visually represent something that we've done wrong. The 40 days of Lent are all about penance.

During the Middle Ages, God came before

the state, and the Vatican would act as a proxy international policy maker, which European rulers were expected to follow. In 1077, Henry IV, The King of Germany, got himself into a spat with The Pope Gregory VII, over what would be known as the *Investiture Controversy*. Gregory, who believed he was the voice of God, circulated a *Papal Dictation* that set out 27 rules, which granted Papal supremacy. Number 3 of those 27 directives was that *'The Pope alone can depose or reinstate bishops'*. Bishops had many powers within a state, but they were often spies for the Pope in foreign lands. Henry, took umbrage at this directive, insisting it was his right to pick or 'invest' the clergymen of his choosing, a precedence that was well established for European state leaders. In his refusal to comply, Gregory promptly excommunicated him.

As the spat escalated, Henry came under pressure from within his empire by those who were nervous about the Church's power. It became apparent to Henry that he needed to get his excommunication lifted as he was losing the political battle both at home and with the Church. In order to get through this tricky mess, he arranged to meet Gregory in Canossa, Northern Italy. On route, Henry encountered numerous problems and was forced to cross, on foot, what was known as the Alpine Crest in the middle of an unprecedented harsh winter with his wife and son. After months of travel, he eventually reached Canossa. However, the Pope, who was locked into his own dilemma about how to deal with the King, left Henry waiting outside the castle for three-days wearing a hairshirt, the traditional clothing of monks, and what would be deemed as penitent attire.

They finally met and the Pope lifted the excommunication. But this didn't stop the simmering powerplay between them, which would drag Henry into a Civil War at home and earn him a second excommunication. Henry lost the Civil War to his rival, Rudolf of Swabia. But, as luck would have it, Rudolf died in the final battle and his forces squabbled over who would be King, allowing Henry to march to Rome unchallenged, as he gathered another army behind him. Henry entered Rome after another battle and soon took St Peter's, forcing

Gregory to flee for his life.

Ultimately, Henry won, becoming The Holy Roman Emperor for a year as Gregory died a disillusioned man away from his beloved Rome. It's hard not to think that standing in the freezing cold for three days, wearing a hairshirt and doing forced penance hadn't been in the back of his mind as he fought his civil war and then marched on Rome. We all need a bit of luck and motivation, and Henry had plenty of both to latch onto.

Since Henry's walk entered the history books, going to 'Canossa' is not only seen as doing penance, but it comes with the connotation that we've been forced into the action.

Effectively forced to apologise.

Coerced against our will.

This is never going to work.

At best, any action will be short-term and unlikely to last. At worst, no action will take place, instead laying the foundation for bitter ongoing resentment that will one day find an airing.

Our action, or call-to-action, has to come from within as it did for United States Senator,

Robert Byrd—the longest serving Senator in US history, at fifty-one years. Over time, Byrd became a highly skilled and deeply respected politician, but his career got off to what can only be called an uncertain start. After seeing his adoptive father march in a Ku Klux Klan parade, the seeds of their messaging took hold and resonated within Byrd. When he was 23-years old, Byrd wrote to one of the Klan's Grand Dragons near where he lived. To Byrd's delight, he received a personal message from the Dragon, who told Byrd he had what it took to be a leader. Byrd was overwhelmed with the attention and signed up to become a member of the Ku Klux Klan, becoming a dedicated recruiter for the organisation in the process.

This was the 1940s. The US was still deeply divided on race issues and Segregation wouldn't be abolished until 1964. Byrd could have used his youth and the attitudes of the time to defend his position. He could have allowed himself to quietly slip into the proceeding decades, letting maturity distance himself from the person he was and the actions he took at twenty-three.

Time cures everything.

But Byrd took another route.

He apologised for his actions and kept on apologising to the end of his life: "I know now I was wrong. Intolerance had no place in America. I apologised a thousand times... and I don't mind apologising over and over again. I can't erase what happened."

He knew his words, though sincere, were not enough to fix his wrong, and he wasn't interested in penance. He needed an action he could sustain that would lead to permanent change. His decision and his call to action was to become an active member of the *National Association for the Advancement of Coloured People* (NAACP).

When Byrd died in 2010 at the age of 93, the NAACP President and CEO at the time, Benjamin Todd Jealous, summed up Bryd's call to action when he said:

"Senator Byrd reflects the transformative power of this nation. Byrd went from being an active member of the KKK to a being a stalwart supporter of the Civil Rights Act, the Voting Rights Act, and many other pieces of seminal legislation that advanced the civil rights and liberties of our country..."

Whether we are religious or not, none of us want to do our own version of the 'Walk to Canossa'. It will stick in our throats, and any actions we start will be short-lived.

To walk the walk, we have to walk it and do it for a substantial amount of time, so it becomes a habit.

It's what change is about.

It's what an apology or the s-word stands for.

These sustained and ongoing actions are the crème de la crème of what we want to achieve.

If in doubt, remember Senator Robert Byrd.

While he kept apologising, his actions with the NAACP spoke louder than words.

They always do.

Something my stepfather and mother never worked out.

Vintage

The s-word comes at us from pain. Its origin is West Germanic, meaning "sore", and dates back to the 6th Century BC. As it worked its way into Old English, it became "sarig", which again meant "pain", but now "distressed" had been added to its meaning. Once we entered Middle English (1150-1300), it turned into "sory", expanding to incorporate "grief" and "mournful" until it landed as we know it today.

"Sorry".

"I'm sorry that you're in pain. Is there anything I can do?"

"I'm sorry I shouted at you. It won't happen again."

"I'm sorry for your loss. How can I help?"

If we say the s-word and mean it, we're signalling that we're empathic to the pain and distress we, someone else, or a set of events, have caused a fellow human being. There's a power and strength within the sound itself. It resonates within our chest and sits more within our body than our head, its history and longevity somehow reverberating through us. If we blurt it out or scatter it like leaves falling from a tree in autumn, we rob ourselves and others of its historical and emotional value. We literally kill its lineage.

The A-word is far dryer. It's the less emotional relative. The sound of the word never seems to leave the confines of our mind, but that doesn't dilute its importance. "Apology" is derived from the Greek word *apo,* meaning "away from", and *logos,* meaning "speech". The famous *"The Apology of Socrates"* was written by Plato and is the eyewitness account of Socrates' self-defence at his trial for impiety and corruption of the youth of Athens in 399 BC.

However, apology's first real appearance in English didn't happen until much later, around the 16th Century, and its meaning was: "a formal defence against an accusation". As it has moved through the centuries, time has shifted its usage, but only slightly, and it still holds strong to its formal context. An apology is a: "verbal or written expression of regret for a fault or failing."

Taken together, one is more personal, and the other formal.

Technically, "Sorry" is an adjective and "Apology" is a noun.

In modern usage, we tend to interchange their meaning and use, and this interchanging can rob us of our intentions if we're not careful. If we can keep it personal, we will always connect better, and that deeper connection will take us further than a formal approach can ever do.

They can sometimes have an added power when combined together. However, this juxtapositioning is easier said than done and can present the user with a tricky problem. Most of us know that if we are meant to be in formal mode, say a first job interview or an important meeting, then being overly personal will likely make us appear less professional and can even lead to offending the other person. The opposite is true. If we need to make it personal and we are too formal, people will likely find us stiff and cold.

This mixing of being sorry with a formal apology combines well when society has to address an uncomfortable moment in its past. Man's history is a chock-a-block catalogue of horrendous acts: war, genocide, slavery, to name but some. It often falls on the preceding generations, sometimes decades, even centuries later, who have to deal with the legacy and the cleanup required. It took the US House of Representatives until 2008 to formally apologise for slavery. The UK Government were only slightly better when, in 2007, the then Prime Minister, Tony Blair, apologised for Britain's role in the Transatlantic Slave Trade.

Apologies issued retrospectively are, by definition, formal. Yet, for all the good intentions, many believe they miss their mark. This is because they tend to come after sustained pressure by a working group or dedicated organisation and, from the giver's perspective, are meant to draw a line under a chapter in history. Whether these formal apologies for a time-stamp in history work or not, or even if we care, depends on our political and historical views, or if we believe the original offence has somehow stained us.

For the retro A-word to really hit home

and be taken seriously, it needs to adopt more of the s-word's make-up for the receiver to sit up and take notice. This is the ultimate challenge for those retrospective apologies that time complicates so quickly. However, in 2006, the British Government got it right. During World War 1, 306 British Soldiers were executed for desertion and cowardice. During the 1914-1918 War, post-traumatic stress disorder hadn't even entered our vocabulary. For those affected by the horrors of fighting in the trenches, it was called 'shellshock'. It could often be recognised by a distant gaze and a glazing over in a soldier's eyes as their cognitive abilities started to shut down in order to protect them from further trauma. It was the brain's last resort before going catatonic.

    Senior officers at the time, who were mostly from upper-class families or even blue blood, had little empathy or even social understanding of the majority of the men who were under their command. The officers couldn't and didn't want to accept "shellshock" as a serious condition. They were scared it would become an excuse not to fight or 'go over the top', as it was known, to be mowed down by German machine-gun fire. In many ways, "shellshock" threatened the entire command structure of the British Army. Therefore, it was easier and simpler to view 'shellshock' as a gross act of cowardice rather than validate its condition.

As a regular or low-ranking soldier, if you weren't shot or injured, then you had to fight. It was black and white. That decision saw 'shellshocked' men executed for horrors they had not been prepared for or could even contemplate how to emotionally handle before going to war. The majority of English servicemen who fought in WWI were either in their late teens or early twenties.

They were kids.

Eighty-eight years later, the British Government not only apologised for this injustice and blight on its own armed forces, but it pardoned every one of the 306 soldiers who were executed. In doing so, they brought justice and peace to the families and campaigners who had fought long and hard to right this wrong.

Some might say it was too little too late, but the fact that first-generation relatives were still alive to benefit from the apology and that a solid action had taken place to right the wrong elevates it within retrospective apologies. It ticked the three important boxes: reflection on the part of the offender (in this case the institution), an official issuing of an apology, followed by a definitive action. It's the 'action' that is borrowed from the all-important s-word that eases it out of the formality and gives it the kicker it needs to really hit home.

#MeToo and Black Lives Matter have both had a huge impact on our culture and recent history. These movements continue to develop, reverberate, and influence change despite the initial offence which sparked the flames having now passed. Frederick Douglass, the freed slave and abolitionist, in his book of 1855, *My Bondage and My Freedom*, made a poignant observation of powerful movements: "Present organisations may perish, but the cause will go on. That cause has a life, distinct and independent of the organisations, patched up from time to time to carry it forward."

Douglas died in 1895 at the age of 77, but not before he witnessed the American Civil War

(1861 – 1865). The victory of the North saw the abolishment of slavery in December of 1865, seven months after the Civil War ended under what would become the Thirteenth Amendment to the United States Constitution. Douglas's observation was almost a forewarning of what was to come. Abolishment of slavery was one of the key drivers that plunged the North against the South in what would become a vicious civil war that saw hundreds of thousands die as outdated military tactics met new technologies in the art of war. A similar story to WWI, which is why so many died in pointless head-on attacks.

A lesson that can perhaps be taken from #MeToo and Black Lives Matter for the next movement that comes along is justice alone is not enough. The movement has to request the s-word too. They have to sit shoulder-to-shoulder from the start. They have to have the same weight of importance. The s-word re-connects with what we all need to feel and hear, dampening the lust for revenge into reasoned actions of continued change.

Harvey Weinstein became one of the

central focuses of the #MeToo[10] movement and it was the individual actions of Derek Chauvin, a police officer for the Minnesota Police, who triggered the Black Lives Matter movement. Chauvin justified his actions as a 'defender of the peace'.

After Chauvin's trial, the Minnesota Police Chief said that his department had contributed to a "deficit of hope" and that "I am absolutely sorry for the pain, devastation and the trauma that Mr. Floyd's death has left on his family, his loved ones and our community."

What the statement lacks is a defined call to action to prevent a similar incident from occurring again. It's the action or actions that follow the words that are the crucial ingredient if the statement of intent is to reverberate deep within the recipient. This is true whether it be an official apology or the simple s-word.

If a movement grows from the ashes of an

---

10. Me Too was originally started on Myspace in 2006 by sexual assault survivor and activist, Tarana Burke. However, it was Alyssa Milano who posted a message on her Twitter account to encourage survivors of sexual assaults to post status updates with the hashtag #MeToo that kick started the movement.

injustice, then a cry to right that wrong has been sounded loud and clear. What isn't always as clear is the cry for an apology. It should be held as high as the flag for justice. In doing so, it broadens the scope of the movement. It also stops the movement spinning towards righteousness and revenge. And while those leading the charge might not think so in the moment, they need to hear the s-word as much as the victims they are fighting for. It's a way to temperature-gauge what is going on and reconnect with what we all want: justice in the short term, followed by a longer-term change that benefits us all. The formal request (not a demand) for an apology can pry open the door to institutionalism, bigotry, and negative cultures as much as the law of justice.

"The great aim of education", said English philosopher Herbert Spencer, "is not knowledge, but action."

Waiting decades or more for a formal apology might eventually tick the boxes and allow official closure, but it can leave many wanting more. Time and circumstance may mean that this official and formal version is all that is available and that we have to accept it with good grace and move on. But when the next movement arrives, this is their chance to learn from history and ensure it's laid out correctly from the start.

The cry for justice and an apology must sit together.

Brothers in arms.

United we stand.

That way, when it's all over, we can look back and feel comfortable about the justice served and the apology uttered in the same way we do after tasting a good vintage.

It's far better that way than the corked and acidic versions that we are so often served up.

Inside me

It is sometimes easier to be cruel than it is to be kind. That was certainly true of the household I grew up in. The default was about having the last vindictive say. It was never about looking to resolve the problem at hand. It wasn't until I left home that I learned that most things can be worked through if we're willing to invest the time and mental effort required.

The problem with kindness and compassion is it takes far more mental energy than their opposites. Cruelty and sarcasm are easier tools to handle. They can be reached without thinking. We need to be able to carry an awareness of the impact our actions have on those around us. We often forget that our actions and our words can resonate with others, sometimes lasting a lifetime within the other person. "Sticks and stones may break my bones, but words will never hurt me" is utter bullshit. Words can be devastating when weaponised against an individual, and we can all benefit from choosing what we say with more care and attention. It's worth remembering that we never forget how someone makes us feel.

If we do transgress and impact someone negatively, the s-word can break open that mistake and give a person a glide path to healing. It's not hard to find those who have refused to do this, or missed the mark so completely with their attempted apology that we wonder why they bothered in the first place. This doesn't include what has become known as the 'non-apology' or 'fake-apology'. A way to express the s-word without doing it or even indicating that we are going to show any remorse whatsoever, effectively adding a touch of spite to the original crime. For some, it has become a sport within itself. If we're hit with: "I'm sorry you feel that way…" then welcome to the world of the 'non-apology' as we've become another victim to it.

Beyond the poorly constructed and non-apologies that float amongst us, there's one that sits upstairs in the cruelty department. It's the apology that turns the thumbscrews right at the end and squeezes its victim to death like a boa constrictor.

The victim has waited, believing the s-word is coming their way, listening on patiently as others who have been caught up in the storm get something to hang on to. The apology is then finished, and when the dust settles and they dig through the debris of what they've heard, they see they've been left out.

    Missed from the list.

    Deliberately in some cases.

    For the victim, the hollowness that was created within widens even more, potentially revicitimising and retraumatising them all over again. They are not only back to square one but are often in a worse position than before it all started.

    In January 1998, Bill Clinton was the 42nd President of the United States of America. He found himself dragged into a sex scandal over allegations that he had an affair with a twenty-two-year-old intern, Monica Lewinsky. Clinton had endured some rough months leading up to the scandal breaking. He was being sued for sexual harassment by Paula Jones, as well as being investigated for a failed property-development scheme when he had been

Governor of Arkansas. As the scandal around Lewinsky gathered momentum, Clinton kept his silence. The pressure continued, and he held firm, attending a White House press conference on an unrelated topic. He started the press conference as his usual jovial self, but his mood turned as he came to the end of his speech. Stood behind a lectern, he rallied to his own defence in what comes across as an unscripted moment, telling the nation and ultimately the world in no uncertain terms that:

"I want you to listen to me. I'm going to say this again: (Clinton now points his index finger on his right hand and wags it to the rhythm of his own beat) I did not have sexual relations with that woman, Miss Lewinsky. I never told anybody to lie, not a single time; never. These allegations are false. And I need to go back to work for the American people. Thank you."

Throughout that spring and into the summer of 1998, the scandal continued to dog Clinton, driven by the relentless Ken Starr, a lawyer, who had spent over three years heading an independent investigation into Clinton's business dealings and private life. Starr was the dog with the bone and had no intention of letting it go. When secretly recorded tapes of Lewinsky discussing her affair with Clinton to a friend became available, along with a semen-covered blue dress that DNA tests would later match to Clinton, the tide turned against the President. To compound his problems, he had denied the affair under a sworn deposition when giving evidence in the Paula Jones sexual harassment case. Clinton was now forced to testify before the Office of Independent Counsel and a Grand Jury on suspected perjury. On that same evening, after his testimony was concluded, he made a public appearance and apologised... sort of.

"I was asked questions about my relationship with Monica Lewinsky. While my answers were legally accurate (managing expectations), I did not volunteer information. Indeed, I did have a relationship with Miss Lewinsky that was not appropriate. In fact, it was wrong. It constituted a critical lapse in judgment and a personal failure on my part for which I am solely and completely responsible."

If Clinton thought this public statement and the fact that his actions stood within the boundaries of the law were going to ease his troubles, he was wrong. He had grossly miscalculated the situation and the storm he had created.

On 11th September 1998, as the summer came to a close, Congress made Ken Starr's report available to the public. That same morning, Clinton decided to make a public statement at a White House breakfast he was having with religious leaders. His timing was identical to his apology in August and had a tactical feel to it (testimony to the grand jury, followed by a Clinton apology; Congress makes the report public, followed by a Clinton apology).

"I don't think there is a fancy way to say that I have sinned. It is important to me that everybody who has been hurt knows that the sorrow I feel is genuine—first and most importantly, my family, also my friends, my staff, my Cabinet, Monica Lewinsky and her family, and the American people."

Clinton's impeccable timing would rear its head once again. On the 11th December 1998, the Judiciary Committee approved three articles of impeachment against the President. Clinton's response was to step out onto the Rose Garden of the White House on the same day and issue another official apology…

"What I want the American people to know, what I want the Congress to know is that I am profoundly sorry for all I have done wrong in words and deeds."

In his five-hundred-word statement of apology, Monica Lewinsky didn't get a personal mention this time, although technically, she fell into the category of "American people". While he did mention her by name in his September apology, it comes in a long list—a bundled package, if you like. As he continues with his December apology, he quickly reverts to his own personal situation and stresses: "not piety, nor tears, nor wit, nor torment—can alter what I have done. I must make my peace with that."

There were still plenty of tough days ahead of him to test his 'peace', but Clinton would go on to be acquitted of all impeachment charges after a senate trial. The scandal faded, as all scandals do, and Clinton would leave his second term in 2001 as one of the most popular presidents in American history. This paved the way for him to enjoy the privileges of the elite, making millions from the lucrative after-dinner speech circuit as well as other business ventures, including writing a number one best-seller with the fiction writer James Paterson.

Monica Lewinsky wasn't so lucky.

She would be in her late thirties before she found her 'peace'. Her mistake at twenty-two would define her future forever. The moment the scandal broke, her career and the life she had known up to that point was gone for good. She was now officially 'Monica Lewinsky'. She would be riddled with personal shame for years. Although the birth of social media did not happen in 1998, the internet had. Overnight she went from a nobody to a media sensation—bullied, harassed, and humiliated online in what would later be known as cyber-bullying, which is now a criminal offence. She would find herself mentioned in over forty rap songs, the butt of jokes, the girl who created zipper-gate. As she said: "she was seen by many, known by few." She lost her reputation and her dignity in the blink of an eye. Her mother was so concerned about her welfare that she didn't leave her side for months, fearful that her daughter would hit such a low she would take her own life.

Another twenty-two-year-old, Chanel Miller, would have her life redefined, too, when she made that youthful mistake of drinking too much at a Stanford fraternity party. She passed out and woke up in an ER room in the local hospital. It transpired that she had been sexually assaulted behind a dumpster for her mistake. Brock Turner was only caught because two men happened by and noticed that Miller was partially naked and not moving. They chased and caught Turner, who was later arrested and charged.

Miller would now have to endure the glare of a public trial and all that it entailed, her character and personality thrown under the spotlight by heavy-hitting lawyers and private investigators. Her emotional life imploded—shame, anger, and humiliation became her constant companions. At the end of the trial, when Turner had been finally convicted, she read a condensed version of her victim impact statement. It started:

"You don't know me, but you've been inside me, and that's why we're here today."

Turner was a nineteen-year-old Stanford University student who was a competitive swimmer and seemed destined to represent his country at the Olympics. He had attended the same party as Miller, drank too much, and only he will ever know why he did what he did. In Miller's victim statement, she poignantly mentions twice the lack of an apology from Turner. The need for the specifics and acknowledgement was required for her to move on.

"I thought there's no way this is going to trial; there were witnesses, there was dirt in my body, he ran but was caught. He's going to settle, formally apologise, and we will both move on. Instead, I was told he hired a powerful attorney, expert witnesses, private investigators…"

Miller goes on to say:

"And I thought, finally, it is over. Finally, he will own up to what he did, [and] truly apologise. We will both move on and get better. Then I read your statement."

A statement where Turner blamed the drinking culture amongst the Stanford students and the sexual promiscuity that went with it. He admitted that the moment had changed everyone's life. He wished that he could undo what he had done. That he's often "debilitated" to think that his actions had caused so much pain, and there's not a "second" he doesn't regret it. He ends his statement with: "I wish I never was good at swimming or had the opportunity to attend Stanford, so maybe the newspapers wouldn't want to write stories about me."[11]

Twenty years on, Clinton was asked by a reporter on NBC, Craig Melvin, if he'd ever apologised to Lewinsky.

"I apologised to everybody in the world", Clinton said.

"But you didn't apologise to her?"

"I have not talked to her", Clinton replied.

"Do you feel like you owe her an apology?"

"No, I do—I do not. I've never talked to her. But I did say, publicly, on more than one occasion, that I was sorry. That's very different. The apology was public."

---

11. Turner was sentenced to six-months in jail and three-year's probation (he was released after three months due to good behaviour). He will remain on the Sex Offender's list for his entire life.

Miller told Turner that her "independence, natural joy, gentleness, and steady lifestyle I had been enjoying became distorted beyond recognition." Clinton was twenty-seven years Lewinsky's senior when he started their affair and one of the most powerful men in the world at the time. He was perhaps fortunate that #MeToo and Twitter were years away from coming into existence.

Lewinsky, too, lost her independence and natural joy. Her world crumbled around her, and it took more than ten years for her to rebuild it. And that's what happens when you get inside someone.

As my stepfather did to me.

It needs a huge amount of effort, energy, and mental agility to get past the pain. It takes time to get back to that spot of independence and natural joy, and the 'direction' of the apology from the perpetrator can make all the difference.

If it's kept general, its impact stays general.

Clinton is right. A public apology is different from a personal one. The public one lacks the punch. It masquerades as specific, but it stays opaque.

The victim ultimately needs a concrete anchor to latch onto. Anchors that, over time, will turn into solid foundations that enable the victims to move past their point of pain. This doesn't happen when the apology stays in the realm of the general— the family, or the people, or the culture, or at the end of a long list, or lingers too long on the perpetrator's own pain, or appears a tactical move to lessen their own guilt.

The Lewinsky's and the Miller's out there need more.

A lot more.

They need the specifics of the apology to be aimed directly at them because whether deliberate or not, the generalist issues the cruellest apologies of them all.

They give hope where there's none intended.

Part IV

Stick your feet up...

"There are only two mistakes one can make along the road to truth; not going all the way, and not starting."
—Buddha

Sticky-tape and plasters

Before he started school, I used to drop my son off at the nursery three mornings a week. We'd have a giggle en route. These are those small moments that I will cherish into my later years. The nursery I took him to is tucked away and surrounded by residential properties. If you didn't know it was there, you'd miss it. As you turn into the street, the road narrows and slowly curves into an unofficial one-way. This allows you to drop off and pick up at the front of the nursery, as well as park in one of the limited allocated spots if needed. As you drive out of the one-way system, it begins to narrow to the point where the line between the pavement and the road becomes somewhat blurred. This narrowing is only for a short distance, a metre-and-half at most, but the unwritten rule is clear.

    Cars on the right.

    Pedestrians to the left.

    One morning, as I turned onto the road that leads to the nursery, I saw someone walking in the middle of the drive-through, texting on their phone, a toddler at their side. After a couple of steps, they stopped in the centre of the unofficial one-way and finished typing their message before walking on. I was late this morning and didn't give it a second thought other than subconsciously clocking the person, and the toddler in tow.

A few days later, I saw exactly the same thing, but this time, the person had dropped off their toddler and was blocking the path of the car waiting patiently behind them. I had two immediate thoughts: 1) this person was being passive-aggressive, and 2) what was creating the anger for it to play out in this way and in this particular spot?

Again, I didn't give the incident much thought beyond my initial reaction until I became caught up in the mini-drama the following week. On this morning, I dropped off my son, and another car pulled out in front of me. Ahead, the person I had seen a few days before, had dropped off their toddler and was walking and texting. At that initial moment, there was enough room for two cars and a pedestrian to move on. Instinctively, I knew what was about to happen. I think the driver in front of me did, too. They hadn't attempted to pass, which they could have done, but they had waited to play extra safe. Sure enough, the person on the phone took a step to their side and stopped in the middle of the drive-through to continue typing their message.

The driver ahead of me stopped and waited.

They had no choice unless they wanted to be arrested for hit-and-run.

After a few moments, the driver ahead of me became visibly agitated at having to wait.

I watched as the driver in the car in front buzzed down their passenger window to say something to the person who had now shuffled back, but not enough for both of us to pass.

The person texting suddenly looked up and said, "Sorry". It was spat out before the driver had barely made a point and while the person was still half dealing with the message they were typing.

I watched on, wondering what would happen next, the moment making me think of my mother. It is exactly the sort of situation that would play into her battling mentality. The idea that she should have to give way if she felt she shouldn't or didn't have to would piss her off. It reminded me that offence is easily taken if you're looking for it. Again, something I had grown up witnessing on many occasions. My experience from watching my mother argue her way through life is that there is no shortage of people who'll indulge you if that's your game. If you're not careful, you can spend your whole life locked into these pointless, petty battles.

I watched on, the driver in front, still chewing over the moment.

The person texting continued sending their message before finally stepping back and out of the way.

Then the moment passed, and the car in front pulled off. As I followed them out, I could see the driver shaking their head, and I knew why.

Apart from the obvious discourtesy, the s-word that had been fired at them meant nothing. It had failed the test on every level of what a good apology is and what it should do for both the giver and the receiver. Even more disappointing is that the person who had issued it was adding to the demise of the s-word and its power. By throwing it out as an aggressive defence to their behaviour, they continued to dilute its meaning not only within themselves but in the receiver. And the more the s-word becomes diluted, the more it loses its potency. A potency that is being ebbed away more and more in our multi-tasking and over-busy lives. It was just a small incident, another irritation, one we all endure in some way, in some part of our day, but it's another nail in the coffin of the s-word and the gift it can hold for everyone.

One of our core problems in issuing the humble s-word is the idea we'll be worse off if we do than if we don't. We can easily become mired in resentment and cornered by our own immaturity. We become overwhelmed with the idea that we are laying ourselves bare for the world to see. But in reality, we are doing the opposite. We are empowering ourselves. We are, in Esther Perel's words: "the stronger", but not at the expense or the detriment of the other. That's the rest of the sentence for me. It's part of the harmony that the s-word offers. It's a gift for everyone involved—giver and receiver—we are "all" the stronger for it.

The commitment needed in going through the process and issuing the s-word can be a challenge. We can't do it if we're busy texting on our phones, running from one meeting to another, filling our lives with pointless tasks. We must first confront our emotions, then voice the s-word appropriately, following it up with sustainable action. In the modern, digital, and overburdened world, this is simply too much for some. It's easier to ignore what we have to do or just blurt out:

"Sorry, but…"

In doing so, we have to realise that we're denying a valuable tool inherent within us all. It's a tool that needs to be kept sharp and can be used to enhance our lives at any given moment when we have unexpectedly, or perhaps deliberately, crossed a line we now regret. And the core of any regret is an overriding feeling that we should have done something or behaved differently for a given circumstance.

At the door to many deathbeds, people will often want forgiveness. They need to make peace with themselves and the world around them before they say their final goodbye. The issuing of those last-minute s-words or the one big one is a powerful, moving movement for everyone who has witnessed it or has been directly involved.

Forgiveness is about letting go of an incident that feels ingrained into our soul. It's not easy, by any stretch of the imagination, and it takes hard emotional work, but if we want to start the process, we have to start by apologising to ourselves. Whether we are the victim or the perpetrator, it will pry open a door for us to step through, even if it's our last breath.

But why wait for the end?

Why not do it now?

The real Legacy we all leave behind is the impression we park within the people who are close to us. It's not the material things we pass on or the wing of the university that gets named after our financial contribution that counts. It's these inner impressions, these indelible stains of either positive or negative vibes that live forever in the other person, that count. The Stoics believed that a successful life was to have a full table. What they meant by a 'full table' was our family and friends wanted to be with us, dine with us to the end. That Friday night dinner is always full. Brunch is hard to get a reservation because there are just too many, and the time slot isn't long enough. If that is a measure of success, then both my mother and stepfather never experienced it.

But here's the trick—it can't be saved to the end. We have to be brave enough to pepper it with all its sincerity when we trip up as we move through life—because we will trip up if we're functioning in the world and trying to live a life of meaning.

As a father, being able to use the s-word is one of the skills I want to teach my children. It's using their in-built emotional intelligence to help them make better choices, and if we make better choices in our life, then… well… our life is better.

But, I have the same problem that they do.

Unless I show them how to use it and embrace it myself, it will atrophy in both them and me.

"I have to show, not tell", as the writing adage goes.

And it's hard sometimes.

But the more we do it, where appropriate, the more we'll see the payback and the easier it'll become.

It's a gift that's been given to us all.

And it's free.

What are we waiting for?

The last mile

I had grown up in a household where abuse was the norm. It came in multiple streams that each had their peaks and troughs. In order to survive, I learned how to read these moments like a savvy analyst who can predict turns in the financial markets. The sideshow was watching my parents abuse each other and anyone else who happened to fly into their orbs at the wrong time. While my mother held down secretarial jobs throughout her life and would often moonlight during her holiday leave, my stepfather continued his cycle of getting fired from every job he ever had, thanks to his choice of alcohol over family.

Like most living in abusive households, I witnessed the passing of the buck and the lack of taking responsibility as a daily practice. The issuing of the humble s-word and the desire to improve everyone's life within the house was strangled into submission long before it ever had a chance to shine its powerful light of redemption.

I had left home just after my eighteenth birthday to escape the madness, but as my twenties drew to an end, I knew that I needed a sea change or my life would end up in the same dead-end cul-de-sac as my parents. It was a place I had witnessed so many times growing up, and one I knew I didn't want to visit again.

That decision to change, along with having children, are the two top choices of my life. Like any survivor of abuse who has moved into the 'thriver' territory, I believe I am proof of Carl Jung's maxim: "I am not what happened to me, I am what I choose to become." We all have that power within us. Each day is a new opportunity to grow. There have been numerous times when I have tripped over myself on my journey to unpick my past or have often outright failed, but I no longer beat myself up and just keep going to what I know is a better place.

Albeit a bit late, discovering how to use the s-word and mean it has changed my life again. I am no longer a hypocritical 'demander' and a harbinger of resentment if it doesn't come my way. I understand the complexities involved in deciding to say it or not and the power it can unleash if I do.

When I reflect back on my own relationship with my mother, biological father, and stepfather, it was woeful on so many levels. I could fill pages with the tales of their stupidity and abuse, but that was never my intention in writing this book. Neither of them knew how to apologise to each other, themselves, or the world around them, and they refused to step onto the threshold of that door, and it cost them all dearly.

My mother and stepfather are now dead. I don't know about my biological father, but if he's still alive, then he will be in his mid-to-late eighties. If I were to sum up their collective abuse into one word, it would be *abandonment* in all its pernicious forms. The relationship with my biological father ended when I was two. My stepfather never made any effort to get to know me and abandoned me before he even started, but not before laying some hope at my feet that he would be different. The one with my mother effectively ended when I was seven and left at the gates of a boarding school. Despite that, I played this strange game with her for years that basically went "Everything is okay as long as we don't talk about it." It was a strategy I played into my forties but couldn't continue any longer.

I had to stop.

I had my own sanity to think about.

The harsh reality is we had no meaningful relationship, and we had next to nothing in common despite being mother and son. She had no idea how I made my living, what my interests were, and who I was as a person. To make matters worse, she didn't even try to know, too wrapped up in her own narcissistic dramas and pains.

There were, of course, the odd moments of joy and genuine affection. She liked to play cards and she taught me Cribbage and Gin Rummy, and I can still hear her laughter as we cycled through another round of Snap. But these moments were fleeting and only added to the false belief that our relationship was more than it was. In reality, it perpetuated the lie that all was normal and safe—a common theme amongst abused children.

Another one of those rare moments of joy was when she unexpectedly booked a weekend in

Paris. We caught a coach from Victoria Station, the ferry from Dover, and another coach from Calais to Paris. It was January and freezing cold. I was twenty-five. When we visited the Eiffel Tower, she wanted a picture taken by one of the street photographers near a bridge that had a lion as a Sentinel with the Eiffel Tower in the background. I thought it was an odd request, but I was happy to oblige and thought nothing more of it. A couple of weeks after our return, she sent me a double-framed photograph of the picture. In the frame, opposite the picture of my mother and myself, was a picture of her and my biological father taken in the exact same spot. It was a picture taken on the first day of their honeymoon. My father was in a suit, and my mother was in heels, looking beautiful but haunted. My father had been twenty-five when he had married my mother. It's a set of pictures I still have. To this day, I have no idea why she went to all that trouble to get that photograph. It would be easy to put it down to guilt or regret, but I think it was far deeper than that. A remorse that haunted her from the moment my real father walked out of her life. It was the end of her second marriage, and she knew she had driven him away. I think, too, she knew that something wasn't right within her, but she just didn't know how to fix it, other than aggression somehow eased her pain, albeit temporarily.

That's narcissism for you.

After we fell out, my mother saw more and more of her brother and his wife. I will never know the tune and context of those conversations, but a year before she died, he had encouraged her to change her will. The small house she had, she left to his two sons. Two grown men who had only met her twice and didn't attend her funeral. When I was delivered a copy of her new will after her death, it had this clause inserted for my benefit.

"I have omitted my son, SJ Sherwood, from this, my Will, because of his years of ill treatment and his despicable attitude towards me."

My crime was sticking up for myself and not apologising for doing so. I made the correct decision for me and one I had been comfortable with from the beginning. I confronted my emotions and concluded there was no apology to give and no action to follow through. The s-word is a gift and should be shared with due care and attention.

Not everyone can accept it, and there are times when it is best not to go there.

But if you do decide not to go there, it has to be a choice after you have gone through the process. It doesn't count otherwise.

A year later, I unexpectedly received all my mother's old photographs. My uncle had left them in the house, and after it had been sold, the new owner kindly took them to the solicitor, and they miraculously found their way to me. They are a complete record of my childhood, something that I had been led to believe had been destroyed. Like any photograph, they become timestamps in your life. While some don't trigger the best of memories, I respect them as a representation of my history. The strangest album of the collection was the one from my mother's second wedding to my father. This album was another secret she had kept from me, and seeing my father as a younger man was stomach-wrenching. Even more painful to witness was the look in his eye. He was radiating misery. There's not one picture where he's smiling, not even in the photograph from his honeymoon in Paris. I can see in his eyes that he knows he's made a mistake. He knew it wasn't going to last. I'm convinced it's why he couldn't find it within himself to talk about us when I saw him twenty-one years later. The emotional narrative is completely different if we say we left because the other person had an affair, not because we made a mistake from the off.

"Apologist" is a word that came out of Christian theology but has now dropped out of usage. The definition of the word is more for an individual who is out there making an argument for things they believe in. I like the idea of being an apologist for the apology, but we can all play our part and be apologists in our own way.

At the start of this book, I mentioned that I had fallen out with my then girlfriend, someone I couldn't quite shake from my mind. I had a long history of walking away from relationships both personally and professionally. No surprise, considering my history and the models I had inherited. Three years later (I'm a slow learner), I made contact with my ex and uttered my own version of the s-word. The net result of that action is my ex is now my wife, and I have two wonderful children—a boy and a girl.

That's what stepping through the threshold can do.

When I look at them and think how my own guardians treated me, I'm often dumbfounded at the decisions made. However, I've since said some more s-words to myself about those bygone days. The net result is that the legacies I will leave with my children will be poles apart from the ones left within me by those who were closest. That may have always been a given due to the work I have put in, but I have used the s-word to shore up my defences.

"I'm sorry that I was abused. I had no say in the family I was born into. I do, however, have a say in how I react."

I'm sure you get the picture.

How far the humble s-word can take us is up to us.

But I know how far it has taken me.

Should we apologise... hell... yes!

A final note

As I finished this book, my aunt peaceful passed away after a brief and noble fight against cancer. She was ninety-three years old and was still driving four months before she died. Her mind sharp and lucid until the final weeks. When my children were born, she sent them cards on their birthday and Christmas. She never missed one. God bless her. May she rest in peace.

About the Author

SJ Sherwood grew up in a small town in the Midlands. He was always fascinated by the power of storytelling and wanted to be a writer from an early age. He has an MA in Drama from UCL. He is the author of the dystopian trilogy *The Denounced*. *Am I...* is his debut psychological thriller that had 40,000 downloads in the first week of publication.

Apologise... Hell, No! The Power of an Apology in an Entitled World is his first non-fiction title. He has also had a successful career selling software in the financial sector and has worked for several FTSE 100 companies. He lives in London with his wife and two young children. He can be found at

www.sjsherwood.com

www.ingramcontent.com/pod-product-compliance
Lightning Source LLC
Chambersburg PA
CBHW052136070526
44585CB00017B/1844